T0353711

Wisdom
For The
Soul

Book 1

Herb Klingele

BALBOA.PRESS
A DIVISION OF HAY HOUSE

Balboa Press books may be ordered through booksellers or by contacting:

Balboa Press
A Division of Hay House
1663 Liberty Drive
Bloomington, IN 47403
www.balboapress.com
844-682-1282

Because of the dynamic nature of the Internet, any web addresses or links contained in this book may have changed since publication and may no longer be valid. The views expressed in this work are solely those of the author and do not necessarily reflect the views of the publisher, and the publisher hereby disclaims any responsibility for them.

The author of this book does not dispense medical advice or prescribe the use of any technique as a form of treatment for physical, emotional, or medical problems without the advice of a physician, either directly or indirectly. The intent of the author is only to offer information of a general nature to help you in your quest for emotional and spiritual well-being. In the event you use any of the information in this book for yourself, which is your constitutional right, the author and the publisher assume no responsibility for your actions.

Any people depicted in stock imagery provided by Getty Images are models, and such images are being used for illustrative purposes only. Certain stock imagery © Getty Images.

Scripture quotations marked KJV are from the Holy Bible, King James Version (Authorized Version). First published in 1611. Quoted from the KJV Classic Reference Bible, Copyright © 1983 by The Zondervan Corporation.

Print information available on the last page.

ISBN: 979-8-7652-3372-6 (sc)
ISBN: 979-8-7652-3373-3 (e)

Balboa Press rev. date: 08/30/2022

Contents

Journal your feelings daily,
letting the Holy Spirit flow through you.

A Celebration of Sequoyah's Life

Sequoyah Hunter Klingele
October 12th, 2004 - April 6th, 2021

Saturday, April 10th, 2021 10:00 AM
Our Lady of Refuge Catholic Church La Honda, California

Dedication

Sequoyah Hunter Klingele, 50% Native American. A shape-shift, trickster, from the Ojibwe Native American Indian Nation, For the JUST, pay attention with spiritual eyes wide open, be a witness to Sequoyah's presents. For the unjust walking around spiritually blind, witnessed the presence of God's wrath

Sequoyah, an amazing beautiful soul, always goes all the way; he keeps his word, will give it his all, and put himself last for those he cares. Rarely received the same compassion and effort in return. Yet, he continued to give freely, a giver and forgiver, very selfless with his love. He kept pushing forward, not letting this cold world change who he was.

Sequoyah Hunter. 12 October 2004 - 6 April 2021. I love my dad, and when my dad cries from his heart for missing me, it shows how much spiritual love my dad has for me.

Available Soon. "Soul Hunter" "Spiritually Written Through The Holy Spirit"

Message to the Readers

The Holy Spirit is very docile. When you detect a fragrance you have never experienced, you will know that you are in the presence of the Holy Spirit.

"The free soul is rare, but you will feel their spirit – basically you feel good, when you are near or with them, feeling their joy and happiness."

Acknowledgment

God came here handicapped in the flesh, as Jesus Christ our Lord who went to the cross and shed His precious blood for our wretched sins from the beginning of time up until now. Jesus Christ, our Lord, rose from the dead three days later and ascended into heaven, seated at the right hand of God, our Father awaiting to judge the living and the dead. Leaving us with the Holy Spirit that moves throughout the earth, answering our prayers and helping one another. After Jesus Christ rose from the dead and stayed 40 days before ascending into heaven, Jesus appeared to over 550 people in 13 different locations.

Introduction

Be nice to yourself because you're worth it, and God is proud of you. God does not make junk, and God does not make mistakes. It is the year 2022, the year of our Lord Jesus Christ. No worries, no stress; that is a moment of happiness and faith you will not get back. No resentments, no regrets; we cannot turn the clock backward. All we can do is move forward, grow along spiritual lines, and try to do the next right thing.

Right now, everything is okay. The last moment is gone; the next moment is not here yet; stay in the moment, living with the Holy Spirit. If we do good things, good things will happen. If we do bad things, bad things will happen.

Always do more for others than you do for yourself. When is the last time you ask anyone if there's anything you can do for them? And especially tell them that you are proud of them. It can change their life.

Try not to let people, places, or things rent space in your head. You will only give them the keys to your mind to keep you, prisoner, there. There's only room for you and God to light your way with Guardian Angels.

You do not read the Bible; the Bible reads you. BIBLE, basic instruction before leaving earth. EGO, easing God out.

Lust of the flesh, sex outside of marriage. The lust for life, money, or materialistic items. And the pride of life. Where the road is wide and paved with good intentions to hell, and many there go in. The road to heaven is one less traveled. Matthew 19; 23 Then Jesus said to his disciples, "Truly I tell you, it is hard for someone who is rich to enter the kingdom of heaven. 24 Again I tell you, it is easier for a camel to go through the eye of a needle than for someone who is rich to enter the kingdom of God."

Our decisions will determine our eternal destination, either heaven or hell. Lust and greed take; love gives.

Agape is a Greek word for God's love that cannot be explained, wider than from horizon to horizon, deeper than all the oceans, beyond our understanding or comprehension or wildest imagination. And the opposite of God's love is God's wrath. The evil feeling cannot be explained as separation from God for eternity.

Six million sperm cells swim for one egg, a generation before generation; we would have a better chance of winning the lottery 1000 times a day than being here right now. In an oxygen bubble, we live on 13 plates floating on molten lava, the earth's crust approximately 40 miles thick.

Imagine our solar system; our sun and nine planets were created within a 24-hour clock. Earth was created in the last one hour of that clock. Man was created in the previous 10 seconds. Now go out into our unknown Milky Way galaxy and venture into our unknown universe. How long are we here? As compared to eternity?

All the greatest thinkers, including Albert Einstein, admitted there was a grand designer of so much harmony and order that could not have evolved.

Will you take the chance? And God loves you. And then the Prince of the air, the devil, will spiritual blinders on the many that will not understand or believe.

We are praying that you find insight through your journaling of these biblical messages, where you will gain knowledge and wisdom through the grace of God.

Abounding Grace

And God is able to make all grace abound toward you; that ye, always having all sufficiency in all things, may abound to every good work.
2 Corinthians 9:8

FOCUS FOR TODAY
The source of our provision will not run out.
It's His grace that abounds daily.

Bible question for the day. "Paul and Silas were imprisoned during the second missionary journey, but in what city did this happen"?

Most home improvement projects take twice as long because the homeowner has to make at least four trips to the hardware store. The first time is to buy the wrong things. The second time is to buy the wrong size. The homeowner buys one of everything and every size on the third trip. The fourth trip allows them to return all the stuff they did not need.

What would it be like to have exactly what you need for all things at all times to do your work? We cannot even imagine! Yet God promises that when we are doing His excellent work, the work He has given us to do, we will have everything we need. It is called grace. It is not something that we can earn, buy or conjure. It is free from a loving God who wants to give us gifts to do His will. He will be surprised by this as we do His good works. We might not recognize ourselves, but we will recognize Him. His grace abounds and is sufficient for us daily.

The day before Thanksgiving, most others are busy preparing for family gatherings and purchasing items to have a warm meal and get together. It is the loneliest time of the year for some people because they either have no one to celebrate with, or they have never had a blessed holiday season themselves. Reaching out to the lonely-hearted is a gracious God-given gift to do. Keep in mind 25,000 people every day die of starvation on this planet. Keep them in mind, say prayers, and thank God for the blessings you have been given in the holiday season. Because His grace overflows in us, we can also extend this mainly to the needy, hurting, and the lost. When you have God and His grace, you have all you need to give others. We are to be cheerful aswe extend our time, talent, and treasure to those in need.

The answer to today's Bible question is. "Philippi"

Prayer: "Father, help me to look to You for all that I need to do Your will. Thank You for Your gift of grace. Lord, please give me a generousheart that looks out for others' needs. Use me as a consistent conduit, Lord, for your glory. In Jesus name, I pray. Amen."

MORE FROM GOD'S WORD

Acts 20:35
I have shewed you all things, how that so labouring ye ought to support the weak, and to remember the words of the Lord Jesus, how he said, It is more blessed to give than to receive.'"

James 1:17
Every good gift and every perfect gift is from above, and cometh down from the Father of lights, with whom is no variableness, neither shadow of turning.

Philippians 4:19
But my God shall supply all your need according to his riches in glory by Christ Jesus.

2 Corinthians 9:7
Every man according as he purposeth in his heart, so let him give; not grudgingly, or of necessity: for God loveth a cheerful giver.

It is better to grow in grace than gifts.
- *Thomas Watson*

Grace gives where He finds empty hands.
- *Augustine*

5 Minute Journaling

ONE THING I WANT TO REMEMBER ABOUT TODAY'S DEVOTION

_____

_____

_____

_____

TODAY I UNDERSTOOD...

_____

_____

_____

_____

TODAY I'M GRATEFUL FOR...

_____

_____

_____

_____

A Full Heart

**The thief cometh not, but for to steal, and to kill,
and to destroy: I am come that they might have life,
and that they might have it more abundantly.
John 10:10**

FOCUS FOR TODAY

The abundant life is not just ideal; it is possible when
we live our life heeding and embracing God's will.

Bible question for the day. "How many years did Joshua live?"

In the beginning, God created heaven and the earth... After that, everything else was made in China. A man is talking to God. The man says, "God, how long is a million years?" God replies to the man, "to me; it's about a minute." And the man replies. "God, how much is $1 million?" And once again, God replies, "To me, it's a penny." The man then replies, "God, may I have a penny?" God then replies. "Wait a minute."

Our lives are filled with more of everything – responsibilities, choices, options, obligations – yet rarely do we feel full and satisfied. Our days are crammed full of undertakings, but our hearts aren't full of joy and peace. We strive hard, filling our schedule, but it leads us to emptiness and helplessness.

The abundant life seems a distant ideal, something we long for but can't experience. But we can. It is possible. The extraordinary life is not just ideal; it is possible when we live our life heeding and embracing God's will.

Our primary need is to know Christ, grow closer to Him, and know His peace and will each day. You don't have to block out hours of your day to spend in prayer and Bible study. But seek first Him first, His kingdom and His righteousness, and all these things will be given to you as well. (Matthew 6:33 NIV)

We need to invite God's presence and seek Him moment by moment. His peace can transform the way we go through our day, reminding us that we have more than enough of whatever it requires. He is enough to sustain us daily. His grace and provision are enough to keep us going.

The answer to today's Bible question is. "110 years".

Prayer: "Jesus, thank you for the way I can experience a full life and a full heart with you. Thank you for the abundant life you bring into my life. Lord, please guide me daily and reveal your will in my life. Amen."

MORE FROM GOD'S WORD

12 For the word of God is alive and active. Sharper than any double-edged sword, it penetrates even to dividing soul and spirit, joints and marrow; it judges the thoughts and attitudes of the heart.

Psalm 37:3
Trust in the LORD, and do good; so shall you dwell in the land, and truly you shall be fed.

Psalm 37:5
Commit your way to the LORD; trust also in him, and he shall bring it to pass.

Proverbs 3:26
For the LORD shall be your confidence, and shall keep your foot from being taken.

Matthew 6:33
But seek first his kingdom and his righteousness, and all these things will be given to you as well.

Remember that when you leave this earth, you can take with you nothing that you have received - only what you have given: a full heart, enriched by honest service, love, sacrifice, and courage.
- Francis of Assisi

5 Minute Journaling

ONE THING I WANT TO REMEMBER ABOUT TODAY'S DEVOTION

_____

_____

_____

_____

_____

TODAY I UNDERSTOOD...

_____

_____

_____

_____

TODAY I'M GRATEFUL FOR...

_____

_____

_____

_____

A Happy Heart

**A merry heart maketh a cheerful countenance: but
by sorrow of the heart the spirit is broken.
Proverbs 15:13**

FOCUS FOR TODAY

Our greatest joy is found in Christ. Our
security is anchored in Him alone.

Bible question for the day. "Why was Daniel put into the lion's den"?

The taste of a delicious grilled steak. A gorgeous summer sunset projects the Merrill of colors. The sound of a child's laughter. The smell of freshly cut grass. The embrace of someone who loves us.

We all have moments of delight that make our hearts happy. Often our senses are involved and perhaps a pleasant memory associated with whatever we are enjoying.

When our hearts overflow with joy, peace, and hope, our contentment shows in our words, expressions, and actions. Others notice that something deep within us fuels our satisfaction and ask us about the source.

Even when the circumstances spin out of control or cause problems we have not anticipated, we can hold on to our joy and keep the smile on our faces. Our certainty in Christ remains rock & solid no matter how demand swirls around us. We have time to stop and smell the roses, cut a few, and make a bouquet for someone else! The menial task captivates our soul when we have Christ, our most significant source of joy.

So be nice to yourself because you're worth it, and God is proud of you. Don't worry, don't stress; there are moments of faith and happiness you will not get back. We cannot turn the clock backward; all we can do is move forward, growing along spiritual lines trying to do the next right thing. God's joy over you gives you courage for tomorrow's battle. He will never forsake you.

Stay in the moment, and everything will be okay; the last minute is gone the next minute. Don't let people, places, or things rent space in your head. It is only room for God. Let the Holy Spirit flow through you, praying for others and helping others with lovingkindness.

God's gift to us is this life; your gift to God is what you do with this life. Greed and lust take, love gives. It's not how much you collect along your soul's journey; it is who you are and what you are becoming through His grace. We came into this world with absolutely nothing, leaving the same way. And here is a sure bet this is 100% fact you can place your money on this one, we are all going to kick the bucket, and we are all going to stand for judgment in front of Jesus Christ our Lord at the end of this journey. God's joy is your strength today. He is always with you.

The answer to today's Bible question is. "Because Daniel prayed."

Prayer: "God, I sometimes lose sight of what truly makes me happy and satisfied – my relationship with You. Thank you for the peace, joy, and hope You provide today. Thank you, Lord, for being my source of joy and security. Jesus, Thank you that my heart finds contentment and fulfillment in you alone. Amen."

MORE FROM GOD'S WORD

Solomon 2:1
I am the rose of Sharon, and the lily of the valleys.

John 10:10
The thief cometh not, but for to steal, and to kill, and to destroy: I am come that they might have life, and that they might have it more abundantly.

Nehemiah 8:10
Then he said unto them, Go your way, eat the fat, and drink the sweet, and send portions unto them for whom nothing is prepared: for this day is holy unto our Lord: neither be ye sorry; for the joy of the Lord is your strength.

Psalm 16:11
Thou wilt shew me the path of life: in thy presence is fulness of joy; at thy right hand there are pleasures for evermore.

Proverbs 17:22
A merry heart doeth good like a medicine: but a broken spirit drieth the bones.

Matthew 5:8
Blessed are the pure in heart: for they shall see God.

"I am grateful for every precious moment life offers me. It allows me to see the miracle in each experience."
- Emmanuel Dagher

5 Minute Journaling

ONE THING I WANT TO REMEMBER ABOUT TODAY'S DEVOTION

_____

_____

_____

_____

_____

TODAY I UNDERSTOOD…

_____

_____

_____

_____

_____

TODAY I'M GRATEFUL FOR…

_____

_____

_____

_____

_____

A Priceless Inheritance

For the Lord will not cast off his people,
neither will he forsake his inheritance.
Psalm 94: 14

FOCUS FOR TODAY

The most significant inheritance we can have
is the gift of salvation.

Bible question for the day. "What does Paul say may "abound more and more in knowledge and all judgment?"

We've all heard stories about people who receive legacies left by relatives they did not know they had. Maybe you've even received such an inheritance yourself. But for most of us, these kinds of stories remain the plot devices of fiction and fantasy. We may have received a legacy, but it came with the steep price of losing a loved one such as a child, parent, guardian, or partner.

However, the most valuable inheritance we have comes as a free gift. And as the saying goes, salvation is free, but it is not cheap. Our inheritance was secured by the ransom paid when Jesus died on the cross for our sins. We had an unfathomable debt we could not pay; God became man to fulfill our payment once and for all.

As a result, we are heirs in an eternal reward. We have a priceless inheritance that comes in the fullness of joy - evidence of our Father's passionate pursuit and unconditional love for us.

The answer to today's Bible question is. "Love."

Prayer: Father, I don't deserve to be Your heir, but You have adopted me as Your precious child. Help me live worthy of this gift, sharing it freely with those around me. Thank you, Lord, for the gift of eternal life you bestowed upon me. Amen".

MORE FROM GOD'S WORD

Romans 8:17
And if children, then heirs; heirs of God, and joint-heirs with Christ; if so be that we suffer with him, that we may be also glorified together.

Psalm 16:5
The LORD is the portion of mine inheritance and of my cup: thou maintainest my lot.

Ephesians 1:18
The eyes of your understanding being enlightened; that ye may know what is the hope of his calling, and what the riches of the glory of his inheritance in the saints,

Revelation 21:7
He who overcomes will inherit these things, and I will be his God and he will be My son.

Galatians 3:29 NIV
And if ye be Christ's, then are ye Abraham's seed, and heirs according to the promise.

You are more than human. You are a child of God.
- Lawrence E. Corbridge

5 Minute Journaling

ONE THING I WANT TO REMEMBER ABOUT TODAY'S DEVOTION

_____

_____

_____

_____

_____

TODAY I UNDERSTOOD…

_____

_____

_____

_____

TODAY I'M GRATEFUL FOR…

_____

_____

_____

_____

A Spirit of Gratitude

**But let us, who are of the day, be sober, putting
on the breastplate of faith and love; and for
an helmet, the hope of salvation.
1 Thessalonians 5:8**

FOCUS FOR TODAY

Being grateful allows us to see
the beauty of God in any season and situation.

Bible question for the day. "Which Old Testament characters appeared with Jesus at the transfiguration"?

We are often encouraged to be specifically mindful of the many blessings in our lives around the Thanksgiving holiday. Many family gatherings include testimonies around the table about what we are particularly grateful for this year. While this beautiful practice allows us to pause and thank God in a celebration of his goodness, we must also remember that our hearts should be attuned to praise Him year-round. It's good to list our many blessings and reflect on them at that time of year. Our families, friends, loved ones, health, jobs, and homes should not be taken for granted. All the more reason that we should make Thanksgiving a year-round holiday.

With the spirit of gratitude in our hearts, we recognize all that God gives us and lose sight of what we think we want but do not have. Thanksgiving isn't a one-year assessment but a daily posture of gratitude and awareness of God's power. We remember His grace, goodness, mercy, and faithfulness. Quick steps to this habit are pausing day by day, listing down what we are grateful for—reading the bible, journaling, praising, and humbly giving back the glory for all the things God has done in our lives.

Even in the season of dryness, we can thank Him in advance that everything will turn out to be good, and God will use everything for His glory. We may not understand things right now, but He is in control and has more beautiful plans for our future. We can praise Him even in the storm. He is a good Father. We can trust Him in the valley. He is a faithful creator.

The answer to today's Bible question is. "Elijah and Moses."

Prayer: Heavenly Father, I have so much and feel so blessed. Thank you for the abundance of friends, family, and blessings in my life today. Give me a grateful spirit, Lord that will praise you no matter the circumstances. I trust you, Lord, and surrender to you my life. Amen!

MORE FROM GOD'S WORD

Psalm 106:1
"Praise ye the Lord. O give thanks unto the Lord; for he is good: for his mercy endureth forever."

Hebrews 12:28-29
"Wherefore we receiving a kingdom which cannot be moved, let us have grace, whereby we may serve God acceptably with reverence and godly fear."

Psalm 69:30
"I will praise the name of God with a song, and will magnify him with thanksgiving."

Psalm 34:8
"O taste and see that the Lord is good: blessed is the man that trusteth in him."

Psalm 86:12
"I will praise thee, O Lord my God, with all my heart: and I will glorify thy name for evermore."

Psalms 13:5
"But I have trusted in thy mercy; my heart shall rejoice in thy salvation."

"Genuine thankfulness is an act of the heart's affections, not an act of the lips' muscles."
- John Piper

5 Minute Journaling

ONE THING I WANT TO REMEMBER ABOUT TODAY'S DEVOTION

_____

_____

_____

_____

_____

TODAY I UNDERSTOOD…

_____

_____

_____

_____

_____

TODAY I'M GRATEFUL FOR…

_____

_____

_____

_____

_____

A Trustworthy Guide

**He restoreth my soul: he leadeth me in the paths
of righteousness for his name's sake.
Psalm 23:3**

FOCUS FOR TODAY

God knows what's best for us,
so we can trust Him on the path where He leads us.

Bible question for the day. "Who wrote Psalms 23"?

The author of this book experienced being spiritually parched and needing direction. This promise of the Lord brings healing and hope to the broken world.

Because of Who God is, we can trust Him and follow Him. It's not just that He's all-knowing and all-powerful; it's that He loves us and wants what is best for us. He is not only a trustworthy guide but also a compassionate one committed to helping us reach our divine destination.

The route He takes will be consistent with His character and His word. He won't take shortcuts that put you at risk or ask you to walk where He has not been. He won't ask you to send or compromise truth along the way. You may not always be comfortable or travel at the pace you would choose, but something is reassuring about not having to control everything. God knows where He's leading you, so let Him. Seek His will. His way is the right way. He is our shepherd.

The answer to today's Bible question is. "King David."

Psalms 23:1–6. – (A Psalm of David.) The Lord is my Shepherd; I shall not want. He makes me lie down in green pastures; He leads me beside the still waters. He restores my soul; He leads me in the paths of righteousness for His name's sake. Yea, though I walk through the valley of the shadow of death, I will fear no evil; for thou art with me; thy rod and thy staff they comfort me. Thou prepares a table before me in the presence of mine enemies; thou anointest my head with oil; my cup runneth over. Surely goodness and mercy shall follow me all the days of my life, and I will dwell in the house of the Lord forever.

Prayer: "Remind me, Lord, that You know exactly what's ahead of me. I can trust You as my guide to take me through each step on my life's journey. Lead me to the path of righteousness that you prepared for me for your glory. In Jesus' name. Amen"

MORE FROM GOD'S WORD

Jeremiah 29:11
"For I know the thoughts that I think toward you, saith the Lord, thoughts of peace, and not of evil, to give you an expected end.".

Psalm 28:7
"The Lord is my strength and my shield; my heart trusted in him, and I am helped: therefore my heart greatly rejoiceth; and with my song will I praise him."

Psalm 37:3
"Trust in the Lord, and do good; so shalt thou dwell in the land, and verily thou shalt be fed."

Psalm 37:5
"Commit thy way unto the Lord; trust also in him; and he shall bring it to pass.".

Proverbs 3:5
"Trust in the Lord with all thine heart; and lean not unto thine own understanding."

Don't let the blessing of God control your direction; let God who gives you direction, be your Controller.
- T. B. Joshua

5 Minute Journaling

ONE THING I WANT TO REMEMBER ABOUT TODAY'S DEVOTION

_____

_____

_____

_____

_____

TODAY I UNDERSTOOD…

_____

_____

_____

_____

_____

TODAY I'M GRATEFUL FOR…

_____

_____

_____

_____

_____

A Wellspring Within

**For with thee is the fountain of life: in
thy light shall we see light.
Psalms 36:9**

FOCUS FOR TODAY

Jesus is our daily bread and living water. He is our most
significant source of light in the darkest times of our lives.

Bible question for the day. "At what city was Jesus born"?

A 16-year-old boy came home with a brand-new Chevrolet Avalanche, and his parents began to yell and scream, "Where did you get that truck???!!! He calmly told them, "I bought it today." "With what money?" Demanded his parents. They knew what Chevrolet Avalanche cost. "Well, "said the boy, "this one cost me just $15." So the parents began to yell even louder. "Who would sell a truck like that for $15?" They said, "It was the lady up the street," said the boy. I do not know her name – they just moved in. She saw me ride past on my bike and asked me if I wanted to buy a Chevrolet Avalanche for $15." "Oh my goodness!" Moaned the mother, "she must be a child abuser." Who knows what she will do next? John, you go right up there and see what is going on." So the boy's father walked up the street to the house where the lady lived and found her out in the yard calmly planting petunias! He introduced himself as the father of the boy to whom she had sold a new Chevrolet Avalanche for $15 and demanded to know why she did it. "Well, "she said, "this morning, I got a phone call from my husband. (I thought he was on a business trip but learned from a friend he had run off to Hawaii with his mistress and did not intend to come back). He claimed he was stranded and needed cash and asked me to sell his new Chevrolet Avalanche and send him the money. So I did.

There are moments in our lives when we don't know what steps we need to stir. Some choices are confusing. In the darkest times of our lives, we need to find the light and fountain of living water.

Underground springs often provide water for fertile areas even when no water is present on the surface. Sometimes these areas become bald, or swamps, low lands where the water bubbling beneath the ground does not drain away. Vegetation and animal life grow for us there even though it might look surprisingly calm at first glance. Change and growth often occur even when we cannot see them.

The same is true with our spiritual lives. God's Spirit within us provides a wellspring of Living Water to nourish and sustain us. And while we may not feel as though we are becoming more mature or deepening our faith as we walk with the Lord, growth is taking place nonetheless. Our Father provides everything we need to grow. The Spirit is at work even when we cannot see what is happening.

The answer to today's Bible question is. "Bethlehem"

Prayer: "Lord, even when I cannot see Your hand at work, I know that You are in control and providing me with everything I need." I have nothing to fear with You as my foundation. Your peace gives me comfort, security, and strength. Nothing can steal my joy today. In Jesus name. Amen"

MORE FROM GOD'S WORD

Evening, and morning, and at noon, I will pray, and cry aloud; and he shall hear my voice.

Psalm 37:5
"Commit thy way unto the Lord; trust also in him; and he shall bring it to pass.".

Psalm 94:19
"In the multitude of my thoughts within me thy comforts delight my soul."

Psalm 86:17
"Shew me a token for good; that they which hate me may see it, and be ashamed: because thou, Lord, hast holpen me, and comforted me."

"Only living water satisfies the thirsty soul."
- Lailah Gifty Akita

5 Minute Journaling

ONE THING I WANT TO REMEMBER ABOUT TODAY'S DEVOTION

_____

_____

_____

_____

_____

TODAY I UNDERSTOOD…

_____

_____

_____

_____

TODAY I'M GRATEFUL FOR…

_____

_____

_____

_____

All the Time

**For through him we both have access
by one Spirit unto the Father.
Ephesians 2:18**

FOCUS FOR TODAY

God is always there for us when we need Him.
He is always available.

Bible question for the day. "Then the disciple who was a tax collector"?

A prospective husband asks the salesgirl. "Do you have a book called "man, the master of women"? The salesgirl says, "the fiction department is on the other side, sir." This guy comes back from the toilet, when a woman says to him, "hey, you have left your garage door open"!" As a man is zipping up his fly, he says with a big smile, "did you see my big black Hummer?" The woman replies, "no, just a mini Cooper with two flat tires." A woman asked a waiter, "what is this fly doing in my ice cream"? The waiter says, "shivering madam." 2 Corinthians 5:7. – Walk by faith, not by sight

While technology now permits us to call, email, text, and video conference with one another worldwide and even in space, we may not be able to contact everyone we wish to get. World leaders, celebrities, actors, and corporate CEOs usually have filters to ensure that anyone can access them directly. If not, their fans, followers, friends, and opportunists would constantly bombard them with messages.

The only One who truly deserves such a level of authority and privilege has done just the opposite. God makes Himself available and accessible to everyone, everywhere and anytime, 24/7/365. We do not need to go through His staff members, personal assistance, or levels of bureaucracy to talk with Him directly.

God allows us to speak with Him directly. We do not have to make an appointment or call ahead. He is eager and waiting to talk with us, any time and all the time.

Remember that God did not go on vacation and leave anyone in charge. Thank God. The devil has a way of making the unjust feel important with their pride. Thinking they know more than God.

What a wonderful gift to quickly access our Heavenly Father in Spirit and truth. This calls us all the more to be humble and subservient to others as a way of showing loving kindness. Do more for others than you do for yourself. Have you found happiness in your life? Has your life brought joy to others? Be nice to yourself because you are worth it, and God is proud of you. First, nourish your relationship with Christ. The second is to allow the Holy Spirit to overflow His love to others through you.

The answer to today's Bible question is. "The disciple Matthew."

Prayer: "Father, I'm so glad You are there for me all the time. Thank You that I do not have to go through another person or jump through hoops to have direct contact. Lord, help me see the beauty of having access with you and use me to lead others the same way. In Jesus mighty name, I pray. Amen."

MORE FROM GOD'S WORD

Psalms 10:4
"The wicked, through the pride of his countenance, will not seek after God: God is not in all his thoughts."

1 John 2:16
"For all that is in the world, the lust of the flesh, and the lust of the eyes, and the pride of life, is not of the Father, but is of the world."

Proverbs 8:13
"The fear of the LORD is to hate evil: pride, and arrogancy, and the evil way, and the froward mouth, do I hate."

Ephesians 4:2
"With all lowliness and meekness, with longsuffering, forbearing one another in love;"

Romans 5:8
"But God commendeth his love toward us, in that, while we were yet sinners, Christ died for us."

"Though our feelings com

"The greatest comfort in this life is having a close relationship with God."
-David O McKey

"Have a solid relationship with Christ and everything will fall in place for you."
- Samuel Zulu

5 Minute Journaling

ONE THING I WANT TO REMEMBER ABOUT TODAY'S DEVOTION

_____

_____

_____

_____

_____

TODAY I UNDERSTOOD…

_____

_____

_____

_____

_____

TODAY I'M GRATEFUL FOR…

_____

_____

_____

_____

_____

Be a Gift

**Every good gift and every perfect gift is from above,
and cometh down from the Father of lights, with whom
is no variableness, neither shadow of turning.**
James 1:17

FOCUS FOR TODAY

There's a need God wants you to see. Respond to His call.
Be a gift to someone He placed in your heart today.

Bible question for the day. "Mary and Joseph were engaged to be married when he learned that Mary was pregnant. What was his response to this bit of news?"

For all of its holiday spirit, cheer, and joyful celebrations, Christmas time of the year can also be one of the loneliest, most painful seasons. There is enormous pressure placed on us to be jolly, happy, and merry all the time. We see movies, TV shows, cards, and stories with a large happy family. We watch eager shoppers scramble for bargains, excited to buy whatever they choose without seeming to worry about their budgets. But what if your family is far away? Or you don't have many people in your life? What if your budget cannot accommodate even the smallest gift or tiniest ornament? What if you are not sure how you will pay the rent, or for groceries, or cover that heating bill?

If you're serious about reclaiming Jesus as the reason for the season, you must be willing to be Christ to those who need Him most. Look around you and see how you can meet the needs of others as a Christmas gift to the Lord. I thank you, Father, for the indescribable gift of His precious Son, Jesus Christ our Lord.

The holiday seasons are not always the greatest. There is a lot of turmoil and chaos amid families for all the wrong reasons. All we have to do is remember that Jesus Christ, our Lord, was born, our Savior. Who came as the Lamb of God, the next time Jesus comes, he will be coming as a roaring lion, not happy. It will be beyond righteous indignation; there may not be words to describe the rapture, the tribulation of the times we are in. As for prophecies in the Bible and by Jesus Christ, our Lord, all the ducks seem to be in order, but only God knows, not even the angels in heaven. Although if you read the Bible, the word of God, it plainly describes the past, the present, and the future, that lay before us. All the major and minor prophets have prophesied the birth, the crucifixion, and the resurrection of our Lord. As well as plainly telling us about the conditions of the end days. It's not getting any better out there, folks, wake up and smell the thorns; the coronavirus, is God's wake-up call to the world to get ready.

The answer to today's Bible question is. "Joseph's immediate thought was, he wanted to break off the engagement.

Prayer: "Lord, You came for all people. Help me to be Your hands and feet and ministered to the people around me who may be struggling and hurting at this time of year. Amen"

MORE FROM GOD'S WORD

Philippians 4:7
"And the peace of God, which passeth all understanding, shall keep your hearts and minds through Christ Jesus."

John 13:34-35
"A new commandment I give unto you, That ye love one another; as I have loved you, that ye also love one another. By this shall all men know that ye are my disciples, if ye have love one to another."

2 Corinthians 9:6
"But this I say, He which soweth sparingly shall reap also sparingly; and he which soweth bountifully shall reap also bountifully.".

Romans 12:13
"Distributing to the necessity of saints; given to hospitality."

"No one is useless in this world who lightens the burdens of another."
- Charles Dickens

"One of the most important things you can do on this earth is to let people know they are not alone."
- Shannon L. Alder

5 Minute Journaling

ONE THING I WANT TO REMEMBER ABOUT TODAY'S DEVOTION

_____
_____
_____

TODAY I UNDERSTOOD…

_____

TODAY I'M GRATEFUL FOR…

_____

Be Authentic

**He that is faithful in that which is least is faithful also in much:
and he that is unjust in the least is unjust also in much.
Luke 16:10**

FOCUS FOR TODAY

Our private life must shine just like our public ministry.
Be authentic and fear the Lord.

Bible question for the day. "How did Sarah learn that she would have a child"?

Who are you when no one is looking? How do you behave when no one around you knows your name or will likely ever see you again? When you travel, do you act differently than at home? Is there a different attitude toward other people than going through a typical day when on vacation?

Other people and our society often encourage us to present one phase in public and another behind closed doors. However, God desires us to live with purity, integrity, and honesty – the same whether we are at home, at work, at church, or on vacation. It is not only our reputation that is at stake; it is the witness we bear to who Christ is in our lives. When others see us changing our behavior according to where we are, they assume that our faith is only a role, a temporary part of our crowded lives. Today, be a worthy ambassador of Jesus, sharing your authentic faith with everyone around you, no matter the context. Indeed our faithfulness in small things reveals our character and our hearts.

Keep a smile on your face; it is the answer to someone's prayer; so many can smile but do not. Be genuine. Be authentic in the presence of the Lord. Seek to foster excellence and integrity in everything you do. God sees the faithfulness you take heart in small things today. He is preparing more incredible things for you! He will reward your commitment.

The answer to today's Bible question is. "She overheard it." (Genesis 18:10.)

Prayer: "God, I confess that sometimes I act differently depending on where I am and who is around. Help me to represent your Son with truth, grace, and integrity. Holy Spirit, help me be faithful to the things you entrusted me, no matter how small it is. Equi[p me Lord for the greater things you planned ahead of me. Amen."

MORE FROM GOD'S WORD

Hebrews 13:2
"Be not forgetful to entertain strangers: for thereby some have entertained angels unawares."

Psalms 104:24
"O Lord, how manifold are thy works! in wisdom hast thou made them all: the earth is full of thy riches."

Joel 2:13
"And rend your heart, and not your garments, and turn unto the Lord your God: for he is gracious and merciful, slow to anger, and of great kindness, and repenteth him of the evil."

Psalm 101:3
"I will set no wicked thing before mine eyes: I hate the work of them that turn aside; it shall not cleave to me."

5 Minute Journaling

ONE THING I WANT TO REMEMBER ABOUT TODAY'S DEVOTION

_____

_____

_____

_____

_____

TODAY I UNDERSTOOD…

_____

_____

_____

_____

_____

TODAY I'M GRATEFUL FOR…

_____

_____

_____

_____

_____

Be His Voice

Learn to do well; seek judgment, relieve the oppressed, judge the fatherless, plead for the widow.
Isaiah 1:17

Pure religion and undefiled before God and the Father is this, To visit the fatherless and widows in their affliction, and to keep himself unspotted from the world.
James 1:27

FOCUS FOR TODAY

God gives us the strength to stand before those who are weaker. Obey the Lord and defend them.

Bible question for the day. "How many Israelites were there and Gideons successful Army?"

The wife said to her husband. "What are you doing?" The husband then says to his wife. "Nothing." The wife then says. "Nothing...?,. You have been reading our marriage certificate for an hour." The husband then says. "I was looking for the expiration date." Matthew 5:8 – Blessed are the pure in heart; for they shall see God.

When Jesus returned to heaven after His resurrection, He left us with the gift of the Holy Spirit. Christ explained that the Spirit dwells in us and is our advocate and comforter, the divine presence of God communicating on our behalf.

With this kind of advocacy as our model, we are called to speak out for those who may not have a voice or those whose voices cannot be heard. This may be challenging and painful. Others may not like defending those who cannot protect themselves. But God gives us strength to stand before those who would harm those weaker than themselves. It is not about as much as it is about reminding others of God's peace, power, and protection.

Today, look for opportunities to take a stand for God's truth against those who would oppress others. Don't be afraid to stand up. Heed the call, and the Holy Spirit will be there to empower and encourage you along the way.

The answer to today's Bible question is. "There were 300 men and Gideon's army".

Prayer: "Lord, empower me to defend those who need help and give me the wisdom to know how to respond to their oppressors. Amen."

MORE FROM GOD'S WORD

Proverbs 31:8-9
"Open thy mouth for the dumb in the cause of all such as are appointed to destruction. Open thy mouth, judge righteously, and plead the cause of the poor and needy.".

Psalm 140:12
"I know that the LORD will maintain the cause of the afflicted, and the right of the poor."

Luke 4:18
"The Spirit of the Lord is upon me, because he hath anointed me to preach the gospel to the poor; he hath sent me to heal the brokenhearted, to preach deliverance to the captives, and recovering of sight to the blind, to set at liberty them that are bruised,"

2 Timothy 4:2
"Preach the word; be instant in season, out of season; reprove, rebuke, exhort with all long suffering and doctrine."

Ephesians 5:11
"And have no fellowship with the unfruitful works of darkness, but rather reprove them."

"The Bible never tells us to take a leap of faith into the darkness and hope that there's somebody out there. The Bible calls us to jump out of the darkness and into the light. That is not a blind leap. The faith that the New Testament calls us to is a faith rooted and grounded in something that God makes clear is the truth."
- R.C. Sproul

5 Minute Journaling

ONE THING I WANT TO REMEMBER ABOUT TODAY'S DEVOTION

_____

_____

_____

_____

_____

TODAY I UNDERSTOOD...

_____

_____

_____

_____

_____

TODAY I'M GRATEFUL FOR...

_____

_____

_____

_____

_____

Be Made New

And be renewed in the spirit of your mind;
Ephesians 4:23

FOCUS FOR TODAY

Renewing our minds is a moment-by-moment
habit we need to embrace by the power of the Holy Spirit.

Bible question for the day. "How many books in the New Testament of 27 books that the apostle Paul write?

You can't deny the power that someone else's genuinely positive attitude can have on you. It can be a co-worker, family member, friend from church, or even a stranger, but it is contagious if they include joy and confidence in the Lord. Nonetheless, it can be frustrating when struggling through a hard day. If only we had a switch to flip that would change our attitudes instantly. While it is not usually that quick and straightforward, we can still train our minds to filter our thoughts on God's truth. When we focus on God's character and the power of His Word, we directly influence our attitude and, subsequently, our feelings.

Just as it takes 20 minutes for our brains to receive the message from our stomach that we are full, it may take a little while between the digestion of truth and our sense of satisfaction. But it will come if we keep up a steady diet of prayer, Bible study, and service to others. We need to digest the word by meditating on it day and night. The truth we are holding on to can affect the attitude of our minds. This is a powerful aspect of our relationship in Christ that will only be possible when we allow the Holy Spirit to work in our lives. We are called to live by the Spirit by focusing and turning our thoughts to heavenly and eternal.

You are a divine creation, and God made you wonderfully and fearfully. Do we have two things to look forward to or not? We are all going to kick the bucket. And we all have to stand in front of the judgment seat of Jesus Christ our Lord. The decisions we make here and now will determine our destiny either in heaven or hell. And if you believe there is a 6-foot hole waiting at the end of this journey for you, that's it. We are all sinners, and God desires to have a personal relationship with you through Jesus Christ, who paid the penalty of our sin. God's gift to us is life; what we do with this life is our gift to God. God does not make junk. One billion years from now, we will be in one of two places, and the decision we make here and now will determine our destiny. Have you accepted Christ already as your Lord and savior? If not, say the prayers below.

The answer to today's Bible question is. "The apostle Paul was credited through the Holy Spirit for writing 13 books of the New Testament.

Prayer: Dear Lord Jesus, I know that I am a sinner, and I ask for Your forgiveness. I believe You died for my sins and rose from the dead. I turn from my sins and invite You to come into my heart and life. I want to trust and follow You as my Lord and Savior. In Your Name. Amen.

MORE FROM GOD'S WORD

Matthew 7:21
"Not every one that saith unto me, Lord, Lord, shall enter into the kingdom of heaven; but he that doeth the will of my Father which is in heaven."

Isaiah 53:5
"But he was wounded for our transgressions, he was bruised for our iniquities: the chastisement of our peace was upon him; and with his stripes we are healed."

Ephesians 2:8-9
8 For by grace are ye saved through faith; and that not of yourselves: it is the gift of God: — 9 Not of works, lest any man should boast.

Romans 12:2
"And be not conformed to this world: but be ye transformed by the renewing of your mind, that ye may prove what is that good, and acceptable, and perfect, will of God."

Romans 8: 5
"For they that are after the flesh do mind the things of the flesh; but they that are after the Spirit the things of the Spirit."

"God's love supply is never empty."
- Max Lucado

5 Minute Journaling

ONE THING I WANT TO REMEMBER ABOUT TODAY'S DEVOTION

_____

_____

_____

_____

_____

TODAY I UNDERSTOOD...

_____

_____

_____

_____

_____

TODAY I'M GRATEFUL FOR...

_____

_____

_____

_____

_____

Beyond Time

**For a thousand years in thy sight are but as yesterday
when it is past, and as a watch in the night.
Psalms 90:4**

FOCUS FOR TODAY

Our life here on earth is nothing compared
to our life in eternity with Jesus.

Bible question for the day. "Paul was shipwrecked on what island"?

Where has this year gone? Only yesterday, it seemed that the new year had started, and you are beginning a new season of growing closer to the Lord. Then winter melted into spring, and you celebrated the resurrection of Christ at the Easter holiday. Soon the flowers pushed up through the ground and burst into color. Trees unfurled their green canopies, and suddenly you are basking in the joy of summer picnics, hikes, gardens, and holidays.

Then summer gave way to fall, and now here you are, enjoying the cool crisp air and the new season of glorious colors in the autumn art show of reds, goals, yellows, and browns. The holidays are just around the corner, and then before you know it, you will be starting a new year again. Where has the time gone? The speed of life seems to go faster and faster. Today, be thankful that you know where you will spend eternity, beyond the linear flow of time that currently confines you - God's preparing for us in eternity. The best place to be.

God loves you and is proud of you, for you are a divine creation, there has never been one of you, and there will never be another, this is your time, for a calling you may have devoting her life to God and service helping others. The pain suffering you are feeling today is not worth comparing with the glory to be revealed to us. (Romans 8:18). The beauty we see in today's time is nothing compared to the eternity we have with God. That makes our life more hopeful amidst tribulations and pain. Don't lose hope. God is watching over you. He doesn't slumber nor sleep. (Psalm 121:4-5)

May God give you the wisdom you need this week as we number our days incline to His heart and will.

The answer to today's Bible question is. "The island of Malta"

Prayer: "Lord, I want to make the most of the time that You have given me here on earth. Help me to be guided by Your schedule and sense of timing and not my own.

MORE FROM GOD'S WORD

Psalms 102:7
"I watch, and am as a sparrow alone upon the house top."

Psalm 121:4-5
4 Behold, he that keepeth Israel shall neither slumber nor sleep. 5 The LORD is thy keeper: the LORD is thy shade upon thy right hand."

Ephesians 5:16-17
16 Redeeming the time, because the days are evil.
17 Wherefore be ye not unwise, but understanding what the will of the Lord is.

"When you can live forever what do you live for?"
- Stephenie Meyer

Carefully Consider

**Now therefore thus saith the Lord
of hosts; Consider your ways.
Haggai 1:5**

FOCUS FOR TODAY

You will never drift away if you seek God above all else.

Bible question for the day. What is the shortest verse in the Bible?

Do you give "careful thought" to your ways? Or do you usually just go with the flow, follow the crowd, or do what's expected of you? God calls each of us to live a Christ-honoring life by the way we love and serve those around us. God wants us to lay aside the selfish pursuits and personal pleasures that entrap and ensnare us in sin. God wants us to enjoy the freedom that comes from following the example of his son, Jesus Christ.

It's pretty easy, however, even when we are firmly rooted in a church or other community of believers simply to do what everyone else is doing. We end up not seeking the ways we are called to live our life to please God and instead just doing what it takes to fit in, conform, and be accepted by the majority.

Sometimes we have to break away from the herd and follow the path God has for us, not the broad road that everyone else continues to travel. We need to carefully consider what we need and what not to do, even it takes us to the narrow path that leads to righteousness.

What has God been speaking to you lately? Is it forgiveness to someone who hurt you? Or reaching out to someone you know. Does the Spirit remind you to pray for someone? To give to the needy. God's promises are accurate, and we can trust Him. Considering our ways also means repenting, casting our past present struggles, and laying to Him our future hopes. Fixing our gaze upon Him and hearing His voice in our daily pursuit of life.

The answer to today's Bible question is. "John 11:35. "Jesus Wept."

Prayer: Dear God, I want to follow you in all areas of my life. Guide me with your wisdom and discernment to know when to step out in faith apart from the crowd. Amen."

MORE FROM GOD'S WORD

Deuteronomy 13:4
"Ye shall walk after the LORD your God, and fear him, and keep his commandments, and obey his voice, and ye shall serve him, and cleave unto him."

Ezekiel 20:19
"I am the LORD your God; walk in my statutes, and keep my judgments, and do them;"

James 4:7
"Submit yourselves therefore to God. Resist the devil, and he will flee from you."

Acts 5:29
"Then Peter and the other apostles answered and said, We ought to obey God rather than men."

Genesis 6:22
"Thus did Noah; according to all that God commanded him, so did he."

Hebrews 12:2
"Looking unto Jesus the author and finisher of our faith; who for the joy that was set before him endured the cross, despising the shame, and is set down at the right hand of the throne of God."

True success is obeying God.
- John C. Maxwell

You will never go wrong obeying God.
- Charles Stanley

5 Minute Journaling

ONE THING I WANT TO REMEMBER ABOUT TODAY'S DEVOTION

_____

_____

_____

_____

_____

TODAY I UNDERSTOOD...

_____

_____

_____

_____

_____

TODAY I'M GRATEFUL FOR...

_____

_____

_____

_____

_____

Check Your Words

**Set a watch, O Lᴏʀᴅ, before my mouth;
keep the door of my lips.
Psalm 141:3**

FOCUS FOR TODAY

The way we speak reflects our relationship with God.

Bible question for the day. "Do you read the Bible?"

Often we think back over recent conversations and wince. "I can't believe I said that!" "I think I hurt her feelings." "I was just trying to be funny and it backfired." We all have many cringe-worthy moments that we wish we could relive. We look behind our words and we can see that our comment had everything to do with our own security, selfishness, anger, and pain. The power of the tongue is something we need to control.

Did you know that God could help you control what you say? If you ask Him to help you, you will be surprised by its effect on your speech. As we take every thought captive, we also need to take every word that came from our mouth. We are to seek and converse that lead to righteousness, peace, and love. Begin a habit by asking, is this word I'll be saying will build up someone or I might regret it later? Second, have I talked this to God in prayer?

There will be a moment before you speak when you pause to think. You will not be able to find the right words without thinking first. You may just become unusually quiet. Soon, your inner conversation of praise and peace will emerge and what you say. God wants your words to bless and build up those around you. The Psalmist here brings encouragement to us by pleading and asking God's help. In our life, we can't do this apart from the Holy Spirit. Let's dedicate our hearts daily to Him. (Ps. 19:14). "Let the words of my mouth and the meditation of my heart be acceptable in your sight"

The answer to today's Bible question is" No, the Bible reads you".

Prayer: "God, help me only to use my words and blessing of you and the people around me. Lord, protect me from the wiles of the enemy. Make me grow in this area to be a mouthpiece for your glory. Amen."

MORE FROM GOD'S WORD

James 1:26
"If any man among you seem to be religious, and bridleth not his tongue, but deceiveth his own heart, this man's religion is vain."

Psalm 34:13
"Keep thy tongue from evil, and thy lips from speaking guile."

Psalm 39:1
"I said, I will take heed to my ways, that I sin not with my tongue: I will keep my mouth with a bridle, while the wicked is before me."

When the mouth stumbles, it is worse than the foot.
- African proverb

5 Minute Journaling

ONE THING I WANT TO REMEMBER ABOUT TODAY'S DEVOTION

_____
_____
_____
_____
_____

TODAY I UNDERSTOOD...

_____
_____
_____
_____

TODAY I'M GRATEFUL FOR...

_____
_____
_____
_____

Commit Time

Wherefore gird up the loins of your mind, be sober, and hope to the end for the grace that is to be brought unto you at the revelation of Jesus Christ;
1 Peter 1:13

FOCUS FOR TODAY

His presence and grace allow us to love others better.

Bible question for the day. "Who was the first person Jesus visited after His resurrection?"

About this time of year, you may find yourself looking ahead to the summer months. Your schedule seems as though it will get the lighter, and vacation is right around the corner. The school will be out soon, and more people will be enjoying time outdoors. You begin to plan ways to enjoy more leisure time, relax, and spend more time with people you want.

Maybe a better commitment of your time is committing to spend it alone with your Father. After that, you can communicate your time goes a long way in any relationship. Yet the best investment you can have is your relationship with God. You do not only make your requests known to Him, but you also learn to quiet your heart and listen. His spirit within us whispers and guides us in directions we might never choose ourselves. But we can rest in the daily steps we take on our journey when we know Who we are following.

Where do you invest your time these days? This verse reminds us that we set our minds and hope in God and His grace. We need to be mindful and obey God what He wants us to do. How are you spending time with God in solitude and silence? Who are the people in your life right now God wants you to show your love? But first, we need to receive and experience God's love so we can overflow. Don't be afraid to embrace slowing down.

A TRUE STORY

Billy Graham witnessed through reading a story out of Reader's Digest. It was a cold winter snowing night with the wind blowing. A neurosurgeon heard a knock at his door. When he opened the door, there was about an 11-year-old girl standing there. And she asked the doctor if he would not mind coming to her home because her mother was sick. The neurosurgeon does not usually make house calls although the look on his little girl's face he grabbed his coat scarf and hat. Follow the little girl a few houses down. He walked in and found the mother, not in real good shape, and he called an ambulance to pick her up and take her to the hospital. The doctor, in the meantime, said that sure is a nice little good daughter you have! The mother replied, "my daughter died a month ago; her things are over there in the closet." The doctor walked over and opened the closet, and there were the same clothes that the little girl was wearing hanging up in the closet. Beware of strangers; you could be entertaining angels unaware. I believe in angels, the kind that heaven sends; I'm surrounded by angels. But I call them friends.

The answer to today's Bible question is. "Mary".

Prayer: "Father, thank You for my friends in the summer months ahead. Help me to remember to spend time with You. Our relationship is my priority. Help me gaze upon you and your love so I can naturally overflow to others. Amen."

MORE FROM GOD'S WORD

Colossians 3:2
"Set your affection on things above, not on things on the earth."

Proverbs 18:24
"A man that hath friends must shew himself friendly: and there is a friend that sticketh closer than a brother."

Philippians 3:20
"For our conversation is in heaven; from whence also we look for the Saviour, the Lord Jesus Christ:"

"The best gift you can give anyone is to spend quality time with them."
- Laurence Overmire

5 Minute Journaling

ONE THING I WANT TO REMEMBER ABOUT TODAY'S DEVOTION

_____

_____

_____

_____

_____

TODAY I UNDERSTOOD…

_____

_____

_____

_____

_____

TODAY I'M GRATEFUL FOR…

_____

_____

_____

_____

_____

Committed to Prayer

For this cause we also, since the day we heard it,
do not cease to pray for you, and to desire that
ye might be filled with the knowledge of his will
in all wisdom and spiritual understanding;
Colossians 1:9

FOCUS FOR TODAY

Praying for others is a privilege, not a burden.

Bible question for the day. "What type of wood did Noah make his arc with"?

Praying with another person can be a very intimate experience. You are not just sharing words and information with them. You are revealing your beliefs, doubts, struggles, needs, dreams, and desires – well, maybe not all at once! But prayer is a way of bonding individuals and knitting their hearts together toward common goals for God's kingdom.

When we commit to pray for someone else's needs, we are sharing their burden and offering to intercede on their behalf before our Father. God already knows their needs, of course, but our participation through prayer is for our benefit as much as theirs. We are changed when we share at a prayer level site line. Prayer provides this access to the most powerful force in the world. But it also opens a connection of compassion between us.

Are there people in your life right now God is prompting you to pray? Talk them to God. He hears our pleas.

The answer to today's Bible question is. "Gopher wood"

Prayer: I'm so grateful that You communicate with me, Father, and allow me to share my own needs as well as those of others. Give me the heart Lord that prays for others relentlessly. Amen."

MORE FROM GOD'S WORD

Psalm 145:18
"The LORD is nigh unto all them that call upon him, to all that call upon him in truth."

Jeremiah 29:12
"Then shall ye call upon me, and ye shall go and pray unto me, and I will hearken unto you."

Galatians 6:2
"Bear ye one another's burdens, and so fulfil the law of Christ."

"You are never more like Jesus than when you pray for others. Pray for this hurting world."
- Max Lucado

"Every great movement of God can be traced to a kneeling figure."
- D.L. Moody

5 Minute Journaling

ONE THING I WANT TO REMEMBER ABOUT TODAY'S DEVOTION

_____

_____

_____

_____

_____

TODAY I UNDERSTOOD…

_____

_____

_____

_____

_____

TODAY I'M GRATEFUL FOR…

_____

_____

_____

_____

_____

Community

If there be therefore any consolation in Christ, if any comfort of love, if any fellowship of the Spirit, if any bowels and mercies, Fulfil ye my joy, that ye be likeminded, having the same love, being of one accord, of one mind.
Philippians 2:1-2

FOCUS FOR TODAY

God's power enables us to bless and help others in need.

Bible question for the day. "What was it that Jacob had to do to marry Rachel?"

So often, tragedy is what unifies us these days. With violence in our schools and public places, with natural disasters wreaking havoc, and with terrible crimes claiming lives, we come together to mourn, grieve, and regroup. Sometimes we band together to take action and prevent the calamity from happening again. Other times we simply unite to serve, restore, and rebuild.

While unity born of tragedy helps us survive and recover, we do not have to wait until a shared loss to come together as a community. We can show the love of Christ to one another without any reason other than exercising our joyful, obedient hearts.

When we are one in spirit and unified and shared beliefs, we become more potent than any individual. God is among us and promises to bless us with His presence. We can meet one another's needs and experience the transformation from both giving and receiving.

The answer to today's Bible question is. "Jacob had to work seven years for Rachel's father Laban before he could marry Rachel. There are a couple of flip sides to this coin; after working seven years, he has the rights from his father-in-law Laban to marry his youngest daughter Rachel. On the wedding day, the unmarried ladies of the time had to wear veils until after they were married. So getting drunk, Jacob was tricked by his father-in-law Laban. The day's custom was that the oldest daughter was to get married first. And Laban's oldest daughter was Leah. She is not a very good-looking lady; as a matter of fact, she was downright ugly. Laban slipped Leah into Jacob's tent the night of the wedding festivity. When Jacob woke up the following day, he had intercourse with Leah Laban's oldest daughter. So Laban said that if Jacob wanted to marry his youngest daughter Rachel, Jacob would work another seven years. Of which he did so willingly because Rachel was so beautiful, and that was the love of his heart. In the meantime, every time Jacob breathed on Leah, she got pregnant. This is where the 12 tribes of Israel originated from. The story goes on, and it is very interesting to read, and the way it is interpreted through theology is amazing.

Prayer: "Lord, today I want to connect with other people and serve them with your love. Help me unite with others who love you or want to know you. Amen."

MORE FROM GOD'S WORD

Colossians 4:2
"Continue in prayer, and watch in the same with thanksgiving;"

Psalm 102:17
"He will regard the prayer of the destitute, and not despise their prayer."

James 5:14
"Is any sick among you? let him call for the elders of the church; and let them pray over him, anointing him with oil in the name of the Lord:"

"True intercession involves bringing the person, or the circumstance that seems to be crashing in on you, before God, until you are changed by His attitude toward that person or circumstance. People describe intercession by saying, "It is putting yourself in someone else's place." That is not true! Intercession is putting yourself in God's place; it is having His mind and His perspective."
- Oswald Chambers

5 Minute Journaling

ONE THING I WANT TO REMEMBER ABOUT TODAY'S DEVOTION

_____
_____
_____
_____
_____

TODAY I UNDERSTOOD…

_____
_____
_____
_____
_____

TODAY I'M GRATEFUL FOR…

_____
_____
_____
_____
_____

Celebrate Him

"For God so loved the world, that he gave his only begotten Son, that whosoever believeth in him should not perish, but have everlasting life."
John 3:16

FOCUS FOR TODAY

Christ is the reason for this season.

Bible question for the day. "In the song 12 days of Christmas, what is given on the seventh day?"

It was the night before Christmas, and all through the pad, not a hipster was stirring, not even old dad; the chimney hung the children with care In hopes that a squad car would soon be there. It can always be worse.

Keep your powder dry, and whatever you do, do not take any wooden nickels. And Omar, the tent maker from bum bum Egypt, may want to give you a ride on his camel, don't go; it's a trick. You better not cry, you better not pout, because I'm telling you why Santa Claus is coming to town; you better not be naughty, you better be nice, because Santa Claus is checking his list, not only once, but twice. So you better not cry, you better not pout, because I'm telling you why Santa Claus is coming to town. - te Just, kanta ni te? Pls dw ko verify ani te if okay for you! :) update me lang if unsa kay wla ko ka G :)

Today, celebrate the birth of Baby Jesus over 2000 years ago! Amidst all the presents and festivities, the meals and the memories, take time to thank God for the most excellent gift you'll ever receive.

Keep the Christ in Christmas; a Savior was born this day; please go to church and give your tithing to honor God with our blessings.

This season isn't only for celebration but also a moment of reflection. It is to be grateful to the greatest gift we receive—the birth of Jesus. Remember always find a reason to laugh. It may not add years to your life, but it surely will add life to your years.

The answer to today's Bible question is. "Swans a-swimming".

Pray: "Lord, my heart is full of joy as I celebrate Your birth today. Let me reflect on Your love and grace and all our festivities with friends and family. Lord, thank you for being our greatest gift in this life. Amen".

MORE FROM GOD'S WORD

Isaiah 9:6
"For unto us a child is born, unto us a son is given: and the government shall be upon his shoulder: and his name shall be called Wonderful, Counsellor, The mighty God, The everlasting Father, The Prince of Peace."

Luke 2:11
"For unto you is born this day in the city of David a Saviour, which is Christ the Lord."

Matthew 1:22-23
"22 Now all this was done, that it might be fulfilled which was spoken of the Lord by the prophet, saying. 23 Behold, a virgin shall be with child, and shall bring forth a son, and they shall call his name Emmanuel, which being interpreted is, God with us."

Christmas gives us the opportunity to pause and reflect on the important things around us.
- David Cameron

I will honor Christmas in my heart, and try to keep it all the year.
- Charles Dickens

5 Minute Journaling

ONE THING I WANT TO REMEMBER ABOUT TODAY'S DEVOTION

_____

_____

_____

_____

_____

TODAY I UNDERSTOOD…

_____

_____

_____

_____

_____

TODAY I'M GRATEFUL FOR…

_____

_____

_____

_____

_____

Control Your Anger

**Be not hasty in thy spirit to be angry: for anger resteth in the bosom of fools.
Ecclesiastes 7:9**

FOCUS FOR TODAY

Don't give the enemy the foothold today. Choose to forgive.

Bible question for the day. "Which gospel is most concerned with the ministry and identity of the person of Jesus?"

Maybe it's people who cut you off on the highway. Or it could be people who talk or text when you are at the movies. People who constantly complain, certain reality TV shows, and automated customer service phone systems do it for most people. Regardless of your pet peeve, we will have things that set us off and get our blood boiling in a hurry. Whether it's the rudeness of others or practical methods of completing tasks at work, we all have experiences that push our buttons and ignite our anger.

Sometimes we are tempted to retaliate, to return rudeness with rudeness, insult with injury, and the anger of others with our own. But God calls us to a different standard, a different control on our anger thermostat. God wants us to be slow to anger and resolve issues quickly so that we do not give our enemy a foothold or opportunity to create jealousy, resentment, or bitterness. Because once our anger bleeds into those areas, we will probably act on it.

Anger that will fest in our minds and hearts will make us feel defeated and tormented. When we encounter a situation alike, we need to run immediately to God, confess, hear His word and ask wisdom on how to deal with certain people. We need to ask God and allow the Holy Spirit to aid us. Today, do not let anything or anyone cause you to lose your temper. Surrender your emotions to God.

The answer to today's Bible question is. "The book of John.

Prayer: "I want to control my anger, Lord, and not allow it to cause me to sin. Have your way in my heart and mind today. Amen."

MORE FROM GOD'S WORD

John 15:13
"Greater love hath no man than this, that a man lay down his life for his friends."

Proverbs 14:29
"He that is slow to wrath is of great understanding: but he that is hasty of spirit exalteth folly."

James 1:19-20
"19 Wherefore, my beloved brethren, let every man be swift to hear, slow to speak, slow to wrath: 20 For the wrath of man worketh not the righteousness of God."

As long as you live on earth, you won't see the end of injustices. Yet God desires for you to let go of injustices and hold on to His grace. Only He can give you the power to forgive those who have hurt you the deepest.
- Paul Chappell

5 Minute Journaling

ONE THING I WANT TO REMEMBER ABOUT TODAY'S DEVOTION

_____

_____

_____

_____

_____

TODAY I UNDERSTOOD...

_____

_____

_____

_____

_____

TODAY I'M GRATEFUL FOR...

_____

_____

_____

_____

_____

Courageously Obey

"But while he thought on these things, behold, the angel of the Lord appeared unto him in a dream, saying, Joseph, thou son of David, fear not to take unto thee Mary thy wife: for that which is conceived in her is of the Holy Ghost. And she shall bring forth a son, and thou shalt call his name Jesus: for he shall save his people from their sins."
Matthew 1: 20- 21

FOCUS FOR TODAY

Obedience is a daily surrender to God's will.

Bible question for the day. "And what city was Jesus born"?

Engaged to be married, Joseph had big plans for his life with Mary, but Marry became pregnant. He did not know how, but he knew that he was not the father of her baby. He was hurt, and to avoid embarrassment, he decided to break it off with Mary quietly.

An angel came to him in a dream and told him to go ahead with the marriage because Mary's baby was the Son of God by the Holy Spirit. He probably did not understand all of what he heard, but he went ahead with the marriage. Joseph's story tells us of a change in life plans. This happens to all of us. We all have stories of disappointment and heartbreak. Without, we were going one way, and we ended up somewhere else.

Sometimes we can see God's leading, but too often, we are not given a reason. We have to move on and do the best we can, knowing that God's plan might be different from ours. This requires courage and trust. We call upon God to redeem and use our new circumstances, knowing He loves us and knows best. Even with the inside information from the angel, Joseph faced ridicule, loss of reputation, and ostracism. It took courage for him to take on his new family and his new mission in life. Joseph courageously obeyed God.

When you face a critical situation, and you find yourself the weaker vessel, "yell as loud as you can, "Jesus help me." Every 46 seconds in the United States, a lady is being raped. Fear knocked, Faith answered, and nobody was there. The only thing we should fear is God.

Luke 12:5. – But I will forewarn you of home you shall fear; fear God, that after you have been killed, God has the power to cast you into hell; yes, I say unto you, fear God. The devil would like you to fear, although the devil trembles at the name of Jesus Christ our Lord.

What are the things God has been speaking to you lately? Obey Him and trust His power courageously.

The answer to today's Bible question is. "Bethlehem"

Prayer: "God, help me to trust that you are in the middle of all of the events in my life. Help me to obey Your will courageously. Amen."

MORE FROM GOD'S WORD

Ephesians 2:19-22
"19 Now therefore ye are no more strangers and foreigners, but fellowcitizens with the saints, and of the household of God; 20 And are built upon the foundation of the apostles and prophets, Jesus Christ himself being the chief corner stone; 21 In whom all the building fitly framed together groweth unto an holy temple in the Lord: 22 In whom ye also are builded together for an habitation of God through the Spirit."

1 Kings 2:3
"And keep the charge of the Lord thy God, to walk in his ways, to keep his statutes, and his commandments, and his judgments, and his testimonies, as it is written in the law of Moses, that thou mayest prosper in all that thou doest, and whithersoever thou turnest thyself:"

Deuteronomy 5:33
"Ye shall walk in all the ways which the Lord your God hath commanded you, that ye may live, and that it may be well with you, and that ye may prolong your days in the land which ye shall possess."

When we find a man meditating on the words of God, my friends, that man is full of boldness and is successful.
- Dwight L. Moody

If you know that God loves you, you should never question a directive from Him. It will always be right and best. When He gives you a directive, you are not just to observe it, discuss it, or debate it. You are to obey it.
- Henry Blackaby

Maturity comes from obedience, not necessarily from age.
- Leonard Ravenhill

5 Minute Journaling

ONE THING I WANT TO REMEMBER ABOUT TODAY'S DEVOTION

_____

_____

_____

_____

_____

TODAY I UNDERSTOOD…

_____

_____

_____

_____

TODAY I'M GRATEFUL FOR…

_____

_____

_____

_____

Deep Satisfaction

**Thou openest thine hand, and satisfiest
the desire of every living thing.
Psalms 145:16**

FOCUS FOR TODAY

The only one who can quench the thirst in
our soul is the one who made us.

Bible question for the day. "According to the gospel of Matthew, where is Jesus first public sermon take place?"

A restful night's sleep. A delicious meal. A restorative vacation. It's good when both our expectations and our needs Meet. We end up satisfied both by what we need, such as food and rest, and content by the enjoyment of the process. Many meals can provide the nutrition we need and fill our stomachs, but not every meal satisfies us. We often sleep until morning but do not awake as rested and refreshed as we'd like. We return from many vacations, grateful for the time away but still agitated and anxious about our life's responsibilities.

Only God provides us with more profound satisfaction, the peace that passes understanding throughout our endeavors. Whether we have our expectations met or get what we hoped, we can still give thanks and trust that God has provided all we need. We can rest easy, enjoy our meal, and feel our spirits lifted regardless of circumstances. This is the essence of contentment. This is the joy of the Christian life. This is soul satisfaction.

The answer to today's Bible question is. "On the mount."

Prayer: Lord, thank you for reminding me that you alone satisfy my soul. I want more of you, Father, and not anything in this world. Reveal to me the things I'm chasing wrong. I want to be filled in your presence alone. Amen.

MORE FROM GOD'S WORD

Hebrews 4:12
"For the word of God is quick, and powerful, and sharper than any twoedged sword, piercing even to the dividing asunder of soul and spirit, and of the joints and marrow, and is a discerner of the thoughts and intents of the heart."

Psalm 16:11
"Thou wilt shew me the path of life: in thy presence is fulness of joy; at thy right hand there are pleasures for evermore."

Matthew 6:33
"But seek ye first the kingdom of God, and his righteousness; and all these things shall be added unto you."

Real satisfaction comes not in understanding God's motives, but in understanding His character, in trusting in His promises, and in leaning on Him and resting in Him as the Sovereign who knows what He is doing and does all things well.
- Joni Eareckson Tada

Ultimate satisfaction is found not in making much of ourselves but in making much of God
- Author: David Platt

5 Minute Journaling

ONE THING I WANT TO REMEMBER ABOUT TODAY'S DEVOTION

_____

_____

_____

_____

_____

TODAY I UNDERSTOOD…

_____

_____

_____

_____

_____

TODAY I'M GRATEFUL FOR…

_____

_____

_____

_____

_____

Demonstrate Grace

And whosoever shall give to drink unto one of these little ones a cup of cold water only in the name of a disciple, verily I say unto you, he shall in no wise lose his reward.
Matthew 10:42

FOCUS FOR TODAY

Our lives are vessels of His grace to others.

Bible question for the day. "Who was the tax collector that climbed up a tree so he could see Jesus?"

While there is nothing we can do to earn God's favor is clear and Scripture that our actions reflect our faith. What we say, we believe, and what we do must be in alignment if our faith has legs – literally.

Without the behavior to back up our beliefs, we only give lip service.

On the other hand, living reveals something about our priorities and what we value most. We are liars if we say we want to be loving, gracious, and generous but don't practice these traits when given opportunities each day. If we claim we love Jesus and follow Him as our master, but we spend all our time and money on ourselves, our commitment has little substance.

To reflect our Father's love, we must accept what He's done for us. To the extent that we embrace grace, we can then express it to those around us. When we give a cup of cold water to a thirsty child, we are demonstrating the tenderness of the Lord and the compassion of Christ. Our lives are an extension of His grace that we can overflow to others.

Moses and God were golfing one day, and they got to the final hole, between the whole and God was a water trap. So God asked Moses to hand him his iron. Moses says, "I think you should use the putter." God replies, just hand me the iron." God makes his first shot, and it lands in the water. He looks at Moses and says. "Will you go retrieve my bowl?" So Moses walks down to the water, parts the waters, and retrieves his bowl. They continue the same pattern three more times until Moses finally refuses to retrieve the ball. When God goes down to the water to retrieve it, an older couple walk by and say. "We have been watching the entire time who does he think he is God or something?" And Moses replies. "No Tiger Woods."

The answer to today's Bible question is. "Zacchaeus."

Prayer: "Dear Lord, I want my actions to match my words today and every day, and for them both to reflect my faith in You. Help me be sensitive to the people you want me to reach out to in my day-to-day living. Fill me with your love, Lord, and allow me to experience, so that I can overflow for your glory. Amen."

MORE FROM GOD'S WORD

John 14:6
"Jesus saith unto him, I am the way, the truth, and the life: no man cometh unto the Father, but by me."

Ephesians 2:10
"For we are his workmanship, created in Christ Jesus unto good works, which God hath before ordained that we should walk in them."

Ecclesiastes 12:14
"For God shall bring every work into judgment, with every secret thing, whether it be good, or whether it be evil."

"Grace is the voice that calls us to change and then gives us the power to pull it off."
- Max Lucado

"Grace needs to be the air we breathe, the atmosphere we live in, whether in church or in the home."
- Allen Snapp

5 Minute Journaling

ONE THING I WANT TO REMEMBER ABOUT TODAY'S DEVOTION

_____

_____

_____

_____

_____

TODAY I UNDERSTOOD...

_____

_____

_____

_____

_____

TODAY I'M GRATEFUL FOR...

_____

_____

_____

_____

_____

Divine Relief

**Blessed be the Lord, who daily loadeth us with
benefits, even the God of our salvation. Selah.
Psalms 68:19**

FOCUS FOR TODAY

If God gives us the burden,
He also trusts us that we will give it back to Him in surrender.

Bible question for the day. "What city was Abraham originally from"?

If you have ever carried a full backpack, an arm full of grocery bags, or a heavy package to mail, you know the relief that comes when you release your burden. Your muscles relax, your arms tangle, and you can catch your breath. If you have ever been carrying a heavy load and someone came along to help lighten it, you know the kind of gratitude you feel for such assistance.

God provides us with the same kind of relief each day. We continually seem to carry the laundry list of cares and concerns to the new items we will add today; He can lift them all. We do not have to strain, strive, and struggle along. In His power, sovereignty, and wisdom, He knows the leverage points that will help us lift our part of the burden. As Jesus also reminds us, it is light and easy to carry. Today, rest in the knowledge that God bears your burdens.

The answer to today's Bible question is. "Abraham came from the city of Ur"

Prayer: "Dear God, I feel so weighed down by life sometimes. Thank you for carrying my burdens and lightening my load today. Amen."

MORE FROM GOD'S WORD

Luke 21; 11, 16, 18
"11 And great earthquakes shall be in divers places, and famines, and pestilences; and fearful sights and great signs shall there be from heaven. 16 And ye shall be betrayed both by parents, and brethren, and kinsfolks, and friends; and some of you shall they cause to be put to death. 18 But there shall not an hair of your head perish."

Matthew 11:29-30
"29 Take my yoke upon you, and learn of me; for I am meek and lowly in heart: and ye shall find rest unto your souls. 30 For my yoke is easy, and my burden is light."

Psalm 138:7
"Though I walk in the midst of trouble, thou wilt revive me: thou shalt stretch forth thine hand against the wrath of mine enemies, and thy right hand shall save me."

"We should try our best to pour out all the burdens in our spirit by prayer until all of them have left us."
- Watchman Nee

Only good things come from God's hands. He never gives you more than you can bear. Every burden prepares you for eternity."
- Basilea Schlink

5 Minute Journaling

ONE THING I WANT TO REMEMBER ABOUT TODAY'S DEVOTION

_____

_____

_____

_____

_____

TODAY I UNDERSTOOD...

_____

_____

_____

_____

_____

TODAY I'M GRATEFUL FOR...

_____

_____

_____

_____

_____

Do Some Pruning

I am the vine, ye are the branches: He that abideth
in me, and I in him, the same bringeth forth much
fruit: for without me ye can do nothing.
John 15:5

FOCUS FOR TODAY

There's a fruit that awaits after the season of pruning.

Bible question for the day. "How tall was Goliath"?

We tend to think of pruning as painful, and while it may be at times, it's also very refreshing to your soul. There's something very liberating about making space for more of God in your life. With the priorities of your faith as your guide, you get back to basics, remembering how you want to spend your time and resources rather than allowing them to be consumed by everyone else's demands.

Gardeners know that trees require pruning to remain healthy and grow straight. We are the same way. We need to get rid of the possessions, relationships, and responsibilities that are not working, especially the ones that pull us away from God. As we "clean house" within our lives, we may discover new rooms where God is waiting for us. He loves us, and He disciplines us. Jesus is the best gardener of our lives. He supplies and gives us the nutrients we need as a branch. We can cast everything to Him to reveal us areas that need more trimming to bear better fruit.

The answer to today's Bible question is. "As recorded in the Bible, Goliath was approximately 10 foot tall."

Prayer: "Lord, give me wisdom about the obstacles to my faith that I need to print away so I can experience the new growth that comes from spending time with you. Amen."

MORE FROM GOD'S WORD

Psalm 94:12
"Blessed is the man whom thou chastenest, O LORD, and teachest him out of thy law;"

Psalm 119:75
"I know, O LORD, that thy judgments are right, and that thou in faithfulness hast afflicted me."

Proverbs 3:11
"My son, despise not the chastening of the LORD; neither be weary of his correction:"

"Pruning is a Necessary Part of Life. In Order to Move Forward, You Must Let Go." - Cheryl Richardson

"The trees which are pruned, watered and nurtured by caring hands bear the greatest fruit; it is the same with people."
- Bryant McGill

5 Minute Journaling

ONE THING I WANT TO REMEMBER ABOUT TODAY'S DEVOTION

_____
_____
_____
_____
_____

TODAY I UNDERSTOOD…

_____
_____
_____
_____

TODAY I'M GRATEFUL FOR…

_____
_____
_____
_____
_____

Enjoy Your Family

For this cause we also, since the day we heard it, do not cease to pray for you, and to desire that ye might be filled with the knowledge of his will in all wisdom and spiritual understanding; Colossians 1:9

FOCUS FOR TODAY

We are never alone in our Christian walk. God blessed us with a spiritual family to help us carry our burdens.

Bible question for the day. "What was the name of Sarah's son?" (Genesis 17; 19)

Asking others for prayer is not always easy. While we are more than willing to pray for the people in our lives, it feels vulnerable and needy to request that they do the same for us. And yet God's word clearly instructs us to pray as individuals as well as with others. Sharing burdens with others and experiencing God's answers and provisions bond us as a spiritual community in ways that praying provided us.

Praying is our communication to God as we share our hearts' concerns and pleas to Him. Our life may seem smooth or rocky road we need not abhor our opportunity to communion with our creator. To pray for someone and being prayed for is such a blessing.

When we hear of an answered prayer from someone we have been praying for, we rejoice with them and remain aware of God's presence throughout the world. When we can share our needs with others, we feel lighter and even comforted, grateful not to be alone with our burden any longer. God created us as social beings to be in relationships with one another. And as we relate to Him as our Father, He wants us to enjoy the fellowship of our brothers and sisters in Christ. Today, I enjoy being part of the family of God.

The answer to today's Bible question is. "Isaac"

Prayer: "Abba Father, thank You for the many wonderful people in my life. I'm grateful for the ways they ministered to me and asked that I may be a blessing in their lives as well. Help me, Lord, be a blessing to those who are needy, hurting, and expand my territory for your glory. Amen"

MORE FROM GOD'S WORD

Song of songs 8:6
"Set me as a seal upon nine heart thine heart. As a seal upon thine arm; for love is strong as death; jealousy is cruel as the grave; the coals thereof are coals of fire, which has a most vehement flame."

Galatians 6:2
"Bear ye one another's burdens, and so fulfil the law of Christ.".

James 5:16
"Confess your faults one to another, and pray one for another, that ye may be healed. The effectual fervent prayer of a righteous man availeth much."

Church is not an organization you join; it is a family where you belong, a home where you are loved and a hospital where you find healing.
- Nicky Gumbel

5 Minute Journaling

ONE THING I WANT TO REMEMBER ABOUT TODAY'S DEVOTION

_____

_____

_____

_____

_____

TODAY I UNDERSTOOD...

_____

_____

_____

_____

TODAY I'M GRATEFUL FOR...

_____

_____

_____

_____

Fellow Citizens

**Now therefore ye are no more strangers
and foreigners, but fellowcitizens with the
saints, and of the household of God;
Ephesians 2: 19**

FOCUS FOR TODAY

We are all God's children, and our citizenship is in heaven.

Bible question for the day. "By what name is Paul of Tarsus known before he begins his missionary activity"?

As travel and technology continue to shrink the world into a global community, now more than ever, we can explore, understand, and accept the hundreds of diverse cultures that comprise our planet. As we share the good news of Jesus to every nation and love and serve those, who are different from us, just as much as those like us, we realize that we are all brothers and sisters in the same royal family. All of our identities here on earth are tied up in our citizenship in heaven. We have a provision that we need, and we lack nothing.

God created us as men and women in his image, whether born in India or Indiana, Southeast Asia or Africa. As we accept the gift of salvation and commit to following Christ, we share as joint heirs in eternal life. We are called to work together in love as the body of Christ, to appreciate our complimentary differences instead of allowing our contrasts to divide us. Pre-justice and bigotry may always tempt us to fear and judge those different from us. But in the family of God, no one is an outsider, alien, or foreigner. We are all God's children. The Gospel extends us the hope that we need as a precious child of God and we can overflow this hope and grace as co-heirs of Christ.

The answer to today's Bible question is. "Saul."

Prayer: "Father, I want to love others the same way you love me, showing your kindness and compassion to my brothers and sisters. Lord, transform me into a distinct child on you and set me apart while I'm still here on earth. Lord, reveal your truth in my life. I will listen. Amen".

MORE FROM GOD'S WORD

Matthew 25; 21
"Well done, thou good and faithful servant, enter thou into the joy of the Lord."

Matthew 25:21
"His lord said unto him, Well done, thou good and faithful servant: thou hast been faithful over a few things, I will make thee ruler over many things: enter thou into the joy of thy lord."

Philippians 3:20
"For our conversation is in heaven; from whence also we look for the Saviour, the Lord Jesus Christ:"

If you are a Christian, you are not a citizen of this world trying to get to heaven; you are a citizen of heaven making your way through this world.
- Vance Havner

5 Minute Journaling

ONE THING I WANT TO REMEMBER ABOUT TODAY'S DEVOTION

_____
_____
_____
_____
_____

TODAY I UNDERSTOOD…

_____
_____
_____
_____
_____

TODAY I'M GRATEFUL FOR…

_____
_____
_____
_____
_____

Finding Contentment

But godliness with contentment is great gain.
1 Timothy 6:6

FOCUS FOR TODAY

Our contentment solely relies on
Christ, not on our circumstances.

Bible question for the day. "Where did Jesus go to perform the atonement?"

Husband and wife are eating soup. The wife spills soup all over her and says, "oh no, I look like a pig," and the husband replies. "Yes, and you also have soup all over you!" How did an intelligent boy propose to a girl? He took the girl along with him on a boat and said in the middle of the river. "Love me or leave the boat." A little boy was so excited because his mom told him he was getting a baby brother. He repeated that to his teacher every day when he came to school, "I'm getting a brother." One day his mom allowed him to feel the baby's kicks in her belly. The next day he came to school and did not say anything to his teacher, so the teacher asked him what had happened to his brother. The little boy replied, "I think mommy ate him."

When was the last time you let out a sigh of contentment? Paul tells us to give thanks in all circumstances and discover joy beyond how we feel about our events. And he certainly knew a thing or two about challenging circumstances. He was shipwrecked, arrested, beaten, placed in jail, and impoverished.

Many of us are filling the void in our hearts, and the things we want to fill can't fully satisfy us. The conviction that we need reveals our hearts in the areas of being content anchored in our intimacy with God. True contentment is acknowledging Christ's sufficiency, and His power is enough. The opposite of contentment allows us to reflect our hearts in the areas of greediness and materialism. How are you in these areas?

You may have a hard time imagining how anyone in such bleak circumstances could ever be content. But you can. When we tether our hope to Christ, we do not have to rely on our circumstances and moods for satisfaction. We can relax, knowing that our lives have meaning when we live out the purpose we were created.

The answer to today's Bible question is "The garden in Gethsemane."

Prayer: "Father, I have all I need in you. Thank you for providing me with your many blessings this yesterday, today, and tomorrow. Amen."

MORE FROM GOD'S WORD

1 Timothy 6:6-7
"6 But godliness with contentment is great gain. 7 For we brought nothing into this world, and it is certain we can carry nothing out."

2 Corinthians 12:10
"Therefore I take pleasure in infirmities, in reproaches, in necessities, in persecutions, in distresses for Christ's sake: for when I am weak, then am I strong."

Psalm 37:3-4
"3 Trust in the Lord, and do good; so shalt thou dwell in the land, and verily thou shalt be fed. 4 Delight thyself also in the Lord: and he shall give thee the desires of thine heart."

"Contentment is the abiding 'Amen' of our joy. It speaks in the present tense, saying: 'I am tasting and I am seeing that the Lord is good.'"
- Erik Raymond

Finish The Race

Knowing this, that the trying of your faith worketh patience.
James 1:3

FOCUS FOR TODAY

God will give us the strength to face the daily battles He prepares for us. Let's finish the race well. Hold on.

5 Minute Journaling

ONE THING I WANT TO REMEMBER ABOUT TODAY'S DEVOTION

_____

_____

_____

_____

_____

TODAY I UNDERSTOOD...

_____

_____

_____

_____

TODAY I'M GRATEFUL FOR...

_____

_____

_____

_____

Bible question for the day. "Who came to Egypt to ask for food from Joseph"?

Some days it is not easy to keep going. Whether it feels like a bad day where nothing goes right or just another boring repeat of the same old routine, we struggle to stay the course. We began to feel insecure and inadequate, unsure if we could maintain the pace we had been going. We do not have all the answers or feel in control. We get tired and do not know how to make it through the day.

These are times when you must cry out to God, acknowledge our pain and weaknesses, and ask for His power and strength to carry us. We know we cannot do it independently and cannot imagine how we can finish the race. And that is okay – it is not up to us. We have to keep living day by day, stepping out in faith moment by moment. God is our strength and our rock in times of distress and trouble. When we feel weak, defeated, and lose hope as we face day-to-day challenges, God's promises hold our hearts to keep running the race.

It may be tiring to run this race, pause, and pray to finish well. If we get stumble, stand up again and walk. Fight our faith in hope and be faithful even in pain. He sees you.

The answer to today's Bible question is "Joseph's brothers." The ones who sold him into slavery told his father Jacob that a wild beast killed him. The brothers ended up coming back to Egypt for food, not knowing their brother was second in command only next to the Pharaoh.

Prayer: "Lord, I want to stay true to Your path and follow You. Strengthen me when I'm tempted and encourage me when I'm tired. Help me to persevere, one step at a time. Hold me tight, Lord, when the burdens of life consume me. I come to your presence and cast everything into your hands. Amen"

MORE FROM GOD'S WORD

Psalms 23:1
"The LORD is my shepherd; I shall not want."

Deuteronomy 31:6
"Be strong and of a good courage, fear not, nor be afraid of them: for the LORD thy God, he it is that doth go with thee; he will not fail thee, nor forsake thee."

Psalm 34:17
"The righteous cry, and the LORD heareth, and delivereth them out of all their troubles."

"God does not want our faith kept in mothballs, so He sometimes allows trials and testing to come into our lives; the unexpected hardships and heartbreaks that rock us in places we never thought we'd face as a child of God. And it's in those defining moments that we knock off the cobwebs of our everyday faith and face life with a new and improved one that's empowered by God Himself."
- Ron Lambro

5 Minute Journaling

ONE THING I WANT TO REMEMBER ABOUT TODAY'S DEVOTION

_____
_____
_____
_____
_____

TODAY I UNDERSTOOD…

_____
_____
_____
_____

TODAY I'M GRATEFUL FOR…

_____
_____
_____
_____

First Trust

Make me to understand the way of thy precepts:
so shall I talk of thy wondrous works.
Psalms 119:27

FOCUS FOR TODAY

The Holy Spirit will help us understand the things God wants
us to learn. Pause and pray. Meditate His word today.

Bible question for the day. "Who did Abraham have Ishmael with;?

Are you the kind of person who likes to think about a problem a long time before tackling it? Or do you tend to jump in and out first and think later? Regardless of how we usually respond to something we do not understand, we can learn and be transformed by the teaching of God's word. There is beauty in the inerrant word of God. He breathes it.

Sometimes we like to ponder a problem or process circumstances to understand them. While this can be insightful, God wants us to trust Him whether we fully grasp the answer or not. Often we try to meditate to understand, and indeed we gain new insight when we immerse ourselves in God's word through meditation. However, if we try to comprehend and apply first and then reflect, we are letting God know that we are willing to be obedient – that is what we understand above all else – rather than contemplate.

Today, practice what it means to understand God's truth before you meditate on the wonder of it. As we hear God as we study the bible, we need to understand the things He wants us to do, memorize and meditate on it day and night. We may not see what God is doing; we can trust Him that He knows what's best for us even the circumstances are not well.

The answer to today's Bible question is. "Sarah's handmaiden and Hagar."

Prayer: "Lord, sometimes I try to solve problems without considering what You want me to do. Give me the patience to wait on Your timing for the current struggles in my life. Amen."

MORE FROM GOD'S WORD

Psalm 105:2
"Sing unto him, sing psalms unto him: talk ye of all his wondrous works."

Psalm 119:34
"Give me understanding, and I shall keep thy law; yea, I shall observe it with my whole heart."

Psalm 119:125
"I am thy servant; give me understanding, that I may know thy testimonies."

"I believe the Bible is the best gift God has ever given to man. All the good from The Savior of the world is communicated to us through this Book."
- Abraham Lincoln

"The primary purpose of reading the Bible is not to know the Bible but to know God."
- James Merritt

5 Minute Journaling

ONE THING I WANT TO REMEMBER ABOUT TODAY'S DEVOTION

_____

_____

_____

_____

_____

TODAY I UNDERSTOOD…

_____

_____

_____

_____

TODAY I'M GRATEFUL FOR…

_____

_____

_____

_____

Follow His Wisdom

**See then that ye walk circumspectly,
not as fools, but as wise,
Ephesians 5:15**

FOCUS FOR TODAY

God's word is our manual to live a life of wisdom.

Bible question for the day. "When Moses died, who led the people"?

When cooking, you follow a recipe; when traveling, you follow the directions from your GPS or map; when assembling a new cabinet, you follow the instructions. Reading through these sequential steps and acting on the information provided allows us to achieve the results we desire; a delicious cake, a pleasant journey to our destination, and an Astarte piece of furniture.

Too often, however, we forget or overlook the instructions that God has provided for us in His word, the Bible. There we find the most important directions for our life's journey. These aren't just rules and regulations or pleasant suggestions to make us feel better. These are principles of truth about ultimate reality – who we are, how we are made, our purpose in life, the character of God, the power of grace, and so much more. Precepts, promises, and precautions in our Christian walk.

If we want to please our Father, we will follow the wisdom that He has provided. If we live by the word of God, we will ultimately have a joyous and happy free life and a journey of wisdom and knowledge that only came from the word of God and His holy grace provided for us along our journey.

Only God knows our hearts and our intentions. We do not walk in anyone's shoes; therefore, that gives us a reason not to be judgmental. Walking wisely in Jesus also means abiding in Him as we seek Him moment by moment. We are ought to walk in the light and not in the darkness. God desires for us to grow physically, emotionally, mentally, and all the more spiritually.

A guy joins a monastery and takes a vow of silence; he can say two words every seven years. After the first seven years, the elders bring him in and ask for his two words. "Cold floors," he says. They nod and send him away. Seven more years pass. They brought him back in and asked for his two words. He clears his throat and says. "Bad food."

They nod and send him away. Seven more years pass. They bring him in for his two words. "I quit," he says. "That is not surprising," the elders say. "You've done nothing but complain since you got here." Psalms 96; 1. –Oh sing Unto the Lord a new song; sing unto the Lord, all the earth.

The answer to today's Bible question is. "Joshua".

Prayer: "Dear God, thank you for giving me guidelines for living the life you want me to live. Help me to follow your ways and grow in wisdom. Correct me, Lord and lead me into the path of righteousness. Amen."

MORE FROM GOD'S WORD

Proverbs 2:6
"For the LORD giveth wisdom: out of his mouth cometh knowledge and understanding."

James 1:5
"If any of you lack wisdom, let him ask of God, that giveth to all men liberally, and upbraideth not; and it shall be given him."

Matthew 7:24
"Therefore whosoever heareth these sayings of mine, and doeth them, I will liken him unto a wise man, which built his house upon a rock:"

There is nothing more foolish than an act of wickedness; there is no wisdom equal to that of obeying God.
- Albert Barnes

The self-confidence of a Christian is nothing but trusting in his wisdom, thinking he knows every teaching of the Scriptures and how to serve God.
- Watchman Nee

5 Minute Journaling

ONE THING I WANT TO REMEMBER ABOUT TODAY'S DEVOTION

_____

_____

_____

_____

_____

TODAY I UNDERSTOOD…

_____

_____

_____

_____

TODAY I'M GRATEFUL FOR…

_____

_____

_____

_____

_____

For His Glory

Know ye not that ye are the temple of God, and
that the Spirit of God dwelleth in you?
1 Corinthians 3:16

FOCUS FOR TODAY

One way of worshipping the Lord is
honoring Him through our bodies.

Bible question for the day. "Who was Abraham's father"?

What are you putting in your temple today? The apostle Paul tells us that our bodies are made for worship as a place where God lives, as vessels where the Holy Spirit dwells. The problems come up because we do not believe this about ourselves. God sees us as holy – a word we do not often use to describe ourselves. It matters what we are allowed to come inside our "temples." When we participate in unhealthy eating, drinking, entertainment, and relationships, we choose to defile God's temple and tarnish our vessel.

Having this perspective on our bodies, minds, and hearts may help us make better choices. We can honor God in our bodies if we see ourselves as His temple. Our Chrisitan life isn't a competition but daily surrender to the Spirit and dying to the flesh. Today, consider what you eat, what you watch, where you go. Do they honor and build up your temple for God's glory?

Remember God always has a better plan for your life. The reason so-called bad things happen to good people is that God loves us that much. Sometimes, God has to stick us back into the fire to burn the impurities off of this precious piece of gold, "our souls." Until we get enough wisdom and faith to where God will use us for his calling, and then, no matter what life has to throw at us, we now "know" – "God's love for us" Through the wisdom we have experienced, going through our trials and tribulations of life. God uses the worst life experiences for His calling, showing those precious souls the joy and happiness they can feel within their body, mind, soul, and spirit, "keeping God first, and doing God's will to help others." God desires you to be holy. Obey Him today.

The answer to today's Bible question is. "Terah."

Prayer: "God, thank You for living inside of me. Help me honor You in my body, mind, and heart by choosing the best way available to me. Remove any impurities in my mind and unholy emotions in my heart. I want to honor you, Lord. Give me strength to be blameless and pure in your sight. Amen."

MORE FROM GOD'S WORD

Peter 2:4-5
"As you come to him, a living stone rejected by men but in the sight of God chosen and precious, you yourselves like living stones, are being built up as a spiritual house, to be a holy priesthood, to offer spiritual sacrifices acceptable to God through Jesus Christ."

2 Corinthians 5:17
"Therefore if any man be in Christ, he is a new creature: old things are passed away; behold, all things are become new."

2 Timothy 2:22
"Flee also youthful lusts: but follow righteousness, faith, charity, peace, with them that call on the Lord out of a pure"

Holiness, not happiness, is the chief end of man.
- Oswald Chambers

Holiness through Christ's Spirit is the accountability every Christian should be striving towards.
- Monica Johnson

5 Minute Journaling

ONE THING I WANT TO REMEMBER ABOUT TODAY'S DEVOTION

_____

_____

_____

_____

_____

TODAY I UNDERSTOOD...

_____

_____

_____

_____

_____

TODAY I'M GRATEFUL FOR...

_____

_____

_____

_____

_____

Forgive Yourself

There is therefore now no condemnation to them which are in Christ Jesus, who walk not after the flesh, but after the Spirit.
Romans 8:1

FOCUS FOR TODAY

God offers forgiveness to us, and we can extend this forgiveness to ourselves.

Bible question for the day. "The name of God is not mentioned in only one book of the Bible. Which one?"

Condemned buildings and houses usually sit vacant, decaying and falling into further disrepair, waiting until they can be destroyed or demolished. Such sites were eyesores and blemished shadows of their former glory when they were new, strong, firm, and freshly painted. Too often, we treat ourselves like a building that has been condemned instead of like a home that has been renovated and restored. God forgives us, loves us, and brings new life. What is old has passed away; He is doing a new thing in us. But often create an enormous challenge for ourselves simply because we are not willing to forgive ourselves even though God has.

Our standard is undoubtedly not higher than God's. No, His standard is holiness. And through the gift of His Son. Jesus, our Father, provided the ultimate firm foundation of our faith.

God's love is far beyond our comprehension, understanding, or imagination. We cannot even become close to knowing God's love, letting the Holy Spirit work through us, to pray for others, and between one another helping the lesser than thou, we begin to understand and see just the twinkle of God's love revealed through us. When was the last time you celebrated who you are in Christ? You are precious in His sight, wonderfully and perfectly made. Instead, we wallow ourselves in despair, shame and condemnation. God offers us the conviction that leads us to repentance. Thus, we can extend grace to ourselves because Jesus did it for us. We can celebrate our worthiness because His grace abounds to us daily. Learn to recognize His voice today more than the whisper of the enemy. You are accepted and loved by the Lord. Forgive yourself.

The answer to today's Bible question is. "The book of Esther."

Prayer: Most gracious Father, I acknowledge that I am a sinner. I come to your throne and presence asking for forgiveness for all my iniquities.

Thank you, Lord, for there is no condemnation once I am in your arms. I pray you will continue to convict me in areas where I can grow deeper in you. Help me endure, Lord, and finish well in this walk. Give me the strength to forgive myself when needed. I accept your free gift of forgiveness. In Jesus name. Amen.

MORE FROM GOD'S WORD

Revelation 1:3
"Blessed is he that readeth, and they that hear the words of this prophecy, and keep those things which are written therein: for the time is at hand."

2 Corinthians 7:10
"For godly sorrow worketh repentance to salvation not to be repented of: but the sorrow of the world worketh death."

Psalm 139:14
"I will praise thee; for I am fearfully and wonderfully made: marvellous are thy works; and that my soul knoweth right well."

Without the cross, there's only condemnation. If Jesus wasn't executed, there's no celebration.
- LeCrae

5 Minute Journaling

ONE THING I WANT TO REMEMBER ABOUT TODAY'S DEVOTION

_____

_____

_____

_____

_____

TODAY I UNDERSTOOD...

_____

_____

_____

_____

TODAY I'M GRATEFUL FOR...

_____

_____

_____

_____

From Death to Life

But if the Spirit of him that raised up Jesus from the dead dwell in you, he that raised up Christ from the dead shall also quicken your mortal bodies by his Spirit that dwelleth in you.
Romans 8:11

FOCUS FOR TODAY

The Holy Spirit is alive within us and offers us
a fresh start in our Christian walk.

Bible question for the day. "Abraham's wife Sarah, who was her handmaiden of whom she instructed to lay with her husband, Abraham".?

Some days, we can't imagine how we will make it through all the demands we face in our schedule. Our families need us, our bosses and coworkers depend on us, yet we have nothing left to give. We want to rely on God's strength, so we prayed, and somehow our Father gets us through. The next day comes, and we have an opportunity to begin again. If we have been blessed with ample rest from a good night's sleep, we can experience our job, school, and home through new eyes. Our problems don't seem as big and overwhelming. Our spirits feel refreshed and entirely reliant on God. Our minds are sharp and, once again, can focus with clarity.

Our heavenly Father has restored us from death to life. He will continue to bring us new life so that we can accomplish what has been set before us, no matter how daunting. Paul wrote in this verse reminding Christians that we are alive spiritually because the Spirit is within us. Because of the fallen world, our physical bodies are dying because of sin. But because of the Spirit, we will be resurrected. Thus, we are free from any condemnation and slavery. The Holy Spirit can restore us even the darkest area in our life.

God loves us through the blood of Jesus Christ, our Lord, and the Holy Spirit that moves throughout the earth, answering our prayers and helping one another. A life is never without a need, never without a problem, never without a painful moment... but never forgets that we have a loving God who is protecting, guiding, and helping us to attain a meaningful life! No matter how dead you feel spiritually, His forgiveness is available for us to repent and come back at His feet.

The answer to today's Bible question is. "Hagar The mother of Muslim descendants, her son's name, "Ishmael." Sarah had a child at 89 years old, and Abraham was 98 years old; their son's name was "Isaac," Sarah's son the mother of Christianity."

Prayer: Thank you, Lord, that our security is solely tied upon you alone, and no one can truly separate us from your love. I pray that you will continue to allow the Holy Spirit to dwell within us, helping us overcome struggles and restore our hearts in this broken world. Amen.

MORE FROM GOD'S WORD

1 John 3:2
"Beloved, now are we the sons of God, and it doth not yet appear what we shall be: but we know that, when he shall appear, we shall be like him; for we shall see him as he is."

1 Thessalonians 4:16
"For the Lord himself shall descend from heaven with a shout, with the voice of the archangel, and with the trump of God: and the dead in Christ shall rise first:"

Believing that you are the righteousness of God through Christ Jesus and simply receiving the gift of no condemnation gives you the power to go and sin no more.
- Joseph Prince

The Gospel is the news that Jesus Christ, the Righteous One, died for our sins and rose again, eternally triumphant over all his enemies, so that there is now no condemnation for those who believe, but only everlasting joy.
- John Piper

5 Minute Journaling

ONE THING I WANT TO REMEMBER ABOUT TODAY'S DEVOTION

_____

_____

_____

_____

_____

TODAY I UNDERSTOOD...

_____

_____

_____

_____

_____

TODAY I'M GRATEFUL FOR...

_____

_____

_____

_____

_____

Gentle Strength

**Let your moderation be known unto
all men. The Lord is at hand.
Philippians 4:5**

FOCUS FOR TODAY

The way we treat others is also a reflection of our relationship
with Christ. He is coming soon. Be ready.

Bible question for the day. "According to the Beatitudes who will be filled?"

.We often think of gentle people as ones who are sensitive, quiet, reserved, and tentative in the way they approach and interact with those around them. However, the kind of gentleness to which we are called is one grounded in strength, compassion, and service. Gentleness is based on love and remains slow to anger. It does not use power unnecessarily but instead humbly serves others in need. It takes a remarkably strong person to speak and to act with gentleness. You must know who you are in order to let go of having to prove yourself, exercise power over others, or demand the attention of entitlement.

Paul reminded us through this verse that we are ought to be reasonable. Jesus ought to return any time at any moment. So this reminder allows us to obey not out of fear but to be more vigilant and be ready of His coming. Gentleness is not just to be content but also to aim for unity with other believers as we relate to them. Setting our gaze to Christ as we hope for His coming. Today, exercise the strength necessary to be gentle and all you do and all you say. Let others see the Father's tenderness and toughness through you.

A wife was making a breakfast of fried eggs for her husband. Suddenly, her husband burst into the kitchen. "Careful," he said, careful! Put in some more butter! Oh my gosh! You are cooking too many at once. Too many! Turn them! Turn them now! We need more butter. Oh my gosh! Where are we going to get more butter? They are going to stick! Careful. Careful! I said be careful! You never listen to me when you are cooking! Never! Turn them! Hurry up! Are you crazy? Have you lost your mind? Do not forget to salt them. You know you always forget to salt them. Use the! Salt. Use the salt! The salt! The wife stared at him. "What in the world is wrong with you? You think I do not know how to fry a couple of eggs?" The husband calmly replied, "I just wanted to show you what it feels like when I'm driving." Galatians 6:9 "And let us not be weary in well-doing, for in due season, we shall reap if we faint not."

The answer to today's Bible question is. "Those who hunger and thirst for righteousness."

Prayer: "Lord, help me to understand what it means to be gentle to those around me. Show me Your gentleness so that I can reflect it to others. Amen."

MORE FROM GOD'S WORD

1 Corinthians 16:22
"If any man love not the Lord Jesus Christ, let him be Anathema Maranatha."

2 Corinthians 10:1
"Now I Paul myself beseech you by the meekness and gentleness of Christ, who in presence am base among you, but being absent am bold toward you:"

Hebrews 10:37
"For yet a little while, and he that shall come will come, and will not tarry."

"I choose gentleness. Nothing is won by force. I choose to be gentle."
- Max Lucado

5 Minute Journaling

ONE THING I WANT TO REMEMBER ABOUT TODAY'S DEVOTION

_____

_____

_____

_____

_____

TODAY I UNDERSTOOD...

_____

_____

_____

_____

TODAY I'M GRATEFUL FOR...

_____

_____

_____

_____

Gift Givers

**The Lord hath appeared of old unto me, saying, Yea,
I have loved thee with an everlasting love: therefore
with lovingkindness have I drawn thee.
Jeremiah 31:3**

FOCUS FOR TODAY

God can use you to someone in need today.

Bible question for the day. "How did God tell Noah that he could escape God's punishment"?

Sometimes the minor acts of kindness can produce enormous rewards. When someone holds the door open for us, surprises us with a cup of coffee, or says, "thank you" for our help, we feel respected, appreciated, and valued. These little gifts of courtesy and compassion often have a more significant impact than anything anyone can give us.

When we give others the same kinds of gifts, we may have no idea how we impact their day. But the little kindness adds up and reminds each of us – both giving and receiving – of the source of all true gift-giving, our Lord. His heart is indeed unfailing and always present in everything he does. Even if we cannot see or understand what He's doing – remember, His ways are not our ways – we can still know that His kindness remains a crucial ingredient. Today, let your attitude of kindness reflect your Father's kindness to you. You may ask someone, is there anything I can do for you? Or is there anything you need? Anything I can pray for you? Sometimes we can catch more bees with honey.

The answer to today's Bible question is. "Build a large boat."

Prayer: Dear God, thank You for showing me blessings and revealing Your unfailing kindness. Allow me to bless others with the same spirit of generosity. Amen."

MORE FROM GOD'S WORD

Romans 10:13
"For whosoever shall call upon the name of the Lord shall be saved."

2 Corinthians 9:6
"But this I say, He which soweth sparingly shall reap also sparingly; and he which soweth bountifully shall reap also bountifully."

Proverbs 11:25
"The liberal soul shall be made fat: and he that watereth shall be watered also himself."

A lack of generosity refuses to acknowledge that your assets are not really yours, but God's.
- Tim Keller

5 Minute Journaling

ONE THING I WANT TO REMEMBER ABOUT TODAY'S DEVOTION

_____

_____

_____

_____

_____

TODAY I UNDERSTOOD...

_____

_____

_____

_____

TODAY I'M GRATEFUL FOR...

_____

_____

_____

_____

_____

Give Yourself

Give, and it shall be given unto you; good measure, pressed down, and shaken together, and running over, shall men give into your bosom. For with the same measure that ye mete withal it shall be measured to you again.
Luke 6:38

FOCUS FOR TODAY

God blessed us so we can be a blessing to others.

Bible question for the day. "What did God form man from"?

God gave us the gift of His Son, the ultimate present for our salvation. His gift enables us to enjoy the closest of relationships with Him, our Father. Because He loves us so much, He regularly blesses us with gifts of friendship, beauty, and provision. There are no strings attached; we have to accept them to enjoy them. All these temporal gifts we are enjoying should not take place God's space in our heart.

God provides our model of giving. With Christ, we see this model in the flesh. Jesus was never too busy to listen to a child, a leper, a tax collector, a prostitute, or even of Pharisee, the hypocritical religious leaders of the day. He gave of Himself to everyone He encountered, healing them, feeding them, transforming them by the power of His truth. Today, show yourself to those around you the same way Jesus did – with selflessness, compassion, and acceptance.

Fred is 32 years old, and he is still single. One day a friend asked, ". Why aren't you married? Can't you find a woman who will be a good wife?" Fred replied. "I found many women I wanted to marry, but when I bring them home to meet my parents, my mother doesn't like them." His friend thinks for a moment and says. "I've got the perfect solution; just find a blonde who is just like your mother." A few months later, they meet again, and his friend says. "Did you find the perfect blonde? Did your mother like her?" With a frown on his face, Fred answered. "Yes, I found the perfect blonde. She would just like my mother. You are right; my mother liked her very much." The friend said. "Then what's the problem?". "Fred replied. "My father doesn't like her." - Proverbs 30:5 Every word of God is pure, God is a shield to those who put their trust in the Lord.

The answer to today's Bible question is. "The dust of the ground".

Prayer: "Lord, You give me so much – thank You! Allow me to give to other people just as generously, pointing them to You as my source. Amen."

MORE FROM GOD'S WORD

Exodus 35:22

"And they came, both men and women, as many as were willing hearted, and brought bracelets, and earrings, and rings, and tablets, all jewels of gold: and every man that offered offered an offering of gold unto the LORD.*"*

Proverbs 19:17

"He that hath pity upon the poor lendeth unto the LORD*; and that which he hath given will he pay him again."*

Psalm 18:2

The Lord is my rock, and my fortress, and my deliverer; my God, my strength, in whom I will trust; my buckler, and the horn of my salvation, and my high tower."

5 Minute Journaling

ONE THING I WANT TO REMEMBER ABOUT TODAY'S DEVOTION

_____

_____

_____

_____

_____

TODAY I UNDERSTOOD...

_____

_____

_____

_____

_____

TODAY I'M GRATEFUL FOR...

_____

_____

_____

_____

_____

God's Profile Never Changes

**Now faith is the substance of things hoped
for, the evidence of things not seen.
Hebrews 11:1**

FOCUS FOR TODAY

We may not see clearly the details of our lives,
God is sovereign and we can trust Him.

Since we have millions of sources online, sometimes it's hard to know who to believe. Years ago, we might have considered most things we saw on the "information superhighway." But with such a growing global online community, it's clear that not everyone can be trusted. From dating sites to start-up business opportunities, many individuals hide behind their virtual identities and deceive others about who they are and what they have to offer. We literally can't accept everyone online at face value because we cannot see them. They might have selfies, profiles, likes, and dislikes, but unfortunately, they may not accurately reveal the online user as a person. It's hard to prod someone with their true identity.

Our faith in God also requires us to make decisions based on limited information. Often we have to risk stepping out in faith, uncertain of the result because of our limited vision. Regardless of the outcome, we can trust that God's profile never changes.

Sometimes it would be easier for us to shrink back, but this verse reminded us to fix our eyes on God and have faith. Looking back to our lives, even at times, it's not easy; we continue to see God's faithfulness and promises unfold in our lives. Just because we can't see things now the way we wanted to be, we trust God's power to continue to reveal even up to eternity. We become more confident and have a dear purposeful faith even in our current afflictions. Even our life here on earth doesn't have fruition as we want to, but as we continue to trust and surrender to God, our lives will make it more fruitful in eternity.

BIBLE - Basic Instructions Before Leaving Earth.

Matthew 7; 13. Enter you in at the strait gate; for wide is the gate, and broad is the way, that leads to destruction, and many there be which go in thereat. 14. –Because straight is the gate, and narrow is the way, which leads unto life, and few there be that find it.

Eternity in one of two places. "Heaven or hell."

The answer to today's Bible question is. "Over 31,000 verses in the Bible".

Prayer: "Lord, I can't see You, but I know You are real. Thank You for all that Your word reveals about You. Strengthen my faith so I can continue to take risks. You want me to take. I want to be where you are, Lord in heaven. Help me endure in my life. Amen."

MORE FROM GOD'S WORD

For in this hope we were saved; but hope that is seen is no hope at all. Who hopes for what he can already see?

2 Corinthians 4:18
"While we look not at the things which are seen, but at the things which are not seen: for the things which are seen are temporal; but the things which are not seen are eternal."

2 Corinthians 5:7
"For we walk by faith, not by sight".

"When I am living with an eternal Kingdom perspective, then growing in relationship with my Creator will rise to the top of my priorities."
- Rachelle Triay

5 Minute Journaling

ONE THING I WANT TO REMEMBER ABOUT TODAY'S DEVOTION

_____
_____
_____
_____
_____

TODAY I UNDERSTOOD…

_____
_____
_____
_____
_____

TODAY I'M GRATEFUL FOR…

_____
_____
_____
_____
_____

Good Fishing

And he saith unto them, Follow me, and
I will make you fishers of men. And they
straightway left their nets, and followed him.
Matthew 4:19 – 20

FOCUS FOR TODAY

Bible question for the day. "Specify the duration which Jonah spent in the abdomen of a giant sea creature"?

You don't have to send a money order for a product advertised on late-night cable TV to know that some items you buy are not the same as what was promised in the commercial. What looked solid, sturdy, technologically advanced, and efficient in the ad seems flimsy, cheap, and time-consuming in actuality. It's a classic example of what is often called "bait and switch." One thing is promised, but something of lesser value is substituted and delivered. And late-night infomercials are not the only ones to use such a tactic. Politicians, corporate leaders, and retail websites have also used this less than the ethical practice of dangling a carrot but delivering a stone.

God never uses the "bait the switch" technique in His relationship with us. It's just the opposite. When we accept the gift of salvation and accept Christ into our hearts, we get more than we ever imagined – an abundant life of purpose and joy in this life and eternal life with God in heaven later.

Keep Jesus Christ our Lord God our Father and the Holy Spirit in mind continuously and pray for those of lesser than us. God can use you mightily according to His ways and will.

The answer to today's Bible question is. "Three nights and three days Jonah spent in the great fish God created specifically for Jonah."

Prayer: "Lord, I want to attract others by the way they see You and what I do and say. I never want to mislead them about the gift of salvation. I'm expectant, Lord to your word and the good works you prepare for me in advance. Amen."

MORE FROM GOD'S WORD

2 Corinthians 9:8
"And God is able to make all grace abound toward you; that ye, always having all sufficiency in all things, may abound to every good work:"

Deuteronomy 28:12
"The LORD shall open unto thee his good treasure, the heaven to give the rain unto thy land in his season, and to bless all the work of thine hand: and thou shalt lend unto many nations, and thou shalt not borrow."

Ephesians 3:20
"Now unto him that is able to do exceeding abundantly above all that we ask or think, according to the power that worketh in us,"

In prayer we can approach God with complete assurance of His ability to answer us. There is no limit to what we can ask, if it is according to His will.
- John F. Walvoord

5 Minute Journaling

ONE THING I WANT TO REMEMBER ABOUT TODAY'S DEVOTION

_____

_____

_____

_____

_____

TODAY I UNDERSTOOD...

_____

_____

_____

_____

_____

TODAY I'M GRATEFUL FOR...

_____

_____

_____

_____

_____

Good Things

Finally, brethren, whatsoever things are true, whatsoever
things are honest, whatsoever things are just, whatsoever
things are pure, whatsoever things are lovely, whatsoever
things are of good report; if there be any virtue, and
if there be any praise, think on these things.
Philippians 4:8

FOCUS FOR TODAY

There is beauty when we behold our thoughts
in His word and goodness.

Bible question for the day. "Who was Joseph's master in Egypt as stated in Genesis 37:36.

With so many graphic, violent images in our lives today, it is no wonder that we often feel anxious and afraid. From video games to cop shows, from advertisements to news stories, we are bombarded with physical pain, human suffering, and disturbing images.

Now more than ever, we must practice the only remedy for our souls; the truth of God's word, the beauty of His creation, and time alone with Him. Once an image is in our minds, we cannot remove it. We can try and forget it, but it is still inside us. The only way to overcome our fear, concern, and shock is to submit it to the Lord.

Today, dwell on the good things that God is doing around you. Meditate on His word and the powerful, positive transformation He is working in your life. Celebrate the beautiful ways He provides for people in need, healing the sick, and comforting the lonely. Dwelling our thoughts, we must fill with holy and good things. We must focus our lives on pleasing God and live His ways. Because of the Holy Spirit, it is possible.

The answer to today's Bible question is. The answer to today's Bible question is. "Potiphar." Genesis 37:36

Prayer: "Jesus, I pray that you would shield my mind from harmful, violent thoughts and help me to dwell on your beauty. Lord, allow me to see the beauty in your word and help me to take every thought captive and make it obedient to you. I want to honor you, Lord, in my thoughts. Help me. In Jesus name. Amen."

MORE FROM GOD'S WORD

Proverbs 30:5
"Every word of God is pure: he is a shield unto them that put their trust in him.".

Romans 14:18
"For he that in these things serveth Christ is acceptable to God, and approved of men."

1 Peter 2:12
"Having your conversation honest among the Gentiles: that, whereas they speak against you as evildoers, they may by your good works, which they shall behold, glorify God in the day of visitation."

"To control your life, control your mind. To control your mind, control your breath."
- Stephen Richards

5 Minute Journaling

ONE THING I WANT TO REMEMBER ABOUT TODAY'S DEVOTION

_____

_____

_____

_____

_____

TODAY I UNDERSTOOD…

_____

_____

_____

_____

_____

TODAY I'M GRATEFUL FOR…

_____

_____

_____

_____

_____

Great Peace

**Great peace have they which love thy law:
and nothing shall offend them.
Psalm 119:165**

FOCUS FOR TODAY

Jesus is our ultimate peace in this chaotic world.

Bible question for the day. The Bible question for the day. "Who found baby Moses"?

When you're anxious and upset, your body reacts accordingly. If you're trying to run away from a perceived threat of imminent danger, you may lose your balance from fear, anxiety, and panic. Your heart will race, and your breathing will become shallow and irregular. Adrenaline will course through your body as it prepares a "fight or flight" response to the threat before you.

When we know the peace of the Lord, however, our entire being experiences the calm tranquillity of knowing our security is in Him. Our body relaxes, we sleep better, and we aren't ruffled by the temporary storm clouds that appear on the horizon. If we follow Jesus and obey God's commands, our feet will remain steadfast and sure. We will not stumble or fall victim to the many worries, fears, and anxieties that try to plague us. Our peace is inevitable. Today, don't let anyone or anything rob you of the security you have been in the Lord.

A wife woke up in the middle of the night to find her husband missing from bed. She got out of bed, checked around the house, and heard sobbing from the basement. After turning on the light and descending the stairs, she found her husband curled up into a bit of ball, sobbing. "Honey, what's wrong?" She asked, worried about what could hurt him so much. "Remember, 20 years ago; I got you pregnant? And your father threatened me to marry you or to go to jail?" "Yes, of course, "she replied. "Well, I would have been released tonight." Ecclesiastes 3; 1.– "To everything, there is a season and time to every purpose under the heaven."

The answer to today's Bible question is. "The Pharaoh's daughter"

Prayer: "Lord, I have nothing to fear with You as my foundation. Your peace gives me comfort, security, and strength. Nothing can steal my joy today. Remove the doubts, anxious thoughts that come along the way. Amen."

MORE FROM GOD'S WORD

Psalm 4:8
"I will both lay me down in peace, and sleep: for thou, LORD, only makest me dwell in safety."

Isaiah 32:17
"And the work of righteousness shall be peace; and the effect of righteousness quietness and assurance for ever."

Proverbs 12:20
"Deceit is in the heart of them that imagine evil: but to the counsellors of peace is joy."

Because of the empty tomb, we have peace. Because of His resurrection, we can have peace during even the most troubling of times because we know He is in control of all that happens in the world.
- Paul Chappell

5 Minute Journaling

ONE THING I WANT TO REMEMBER ABOUT TODAY'S DEVOTION

_____

_____

_____

_____

_____

TODAY I UNDERSTOOD…

_____

_____

_____

_____

_____

TODAY I'M GRATEFUL FOR…

_____

_____

_____

_____

_____

Grow In Grace

But grow in grace, and in the knowledge of
our Lord and Saviour Jesus Christ. To him be
glory both now and for ever. Amen.
2 Peter 3:18

FOCUS FOR TODAY

We cannot grow in grace apart from Christ.

Bible question for the day. "What is the shortest chapter in the Bible?"

At the beginning of the spring, it seems as though nature held its collective breath waiting for the consistency of sunshine, rain, and warm temperatures. Then all at once, trees, feel, and yards deepened into and roll shades of green. While flowers dotted the hillsides and cornfields sprang up. Soon cornstalks towered over 6 feet, trying to keep up with sunflowers. Living creatures grow, and nowhere in this clearer than in the middle of summer. The natural world erupts with color, life, and vibrancy, yielding delicious produce and beautiful blossoms.

When we walk with the Lord and remain nourished by His word, by fellowship with other believers, and by our service to those around us, we also grow and flourish. God wants His children to mature in their faith, trusting Him more and more each day.

This verse is a reminder to grow in the grace of God and knowledge of Him. To live in His grace allow us to grow spiritually even more. To succeed in knowing more of Christ and to grow in our relationship with Him. May we enjoy and grow in our relationship with God.

The answer to today's Bible question is. "Psalms chapter 117". Oh, praise the Lord, all you nations; praise Him, all you people. For His merciful kindness is great towards us; and the truth of the Lord endures forever. Praise You, Lord.

Prayer: "Lord, I want to step out in faith and move beyond my comfort zone. I want others to know how much I love You and how Your grace has transformed my life. Give me boldness, Lord and allow me to live a grace-filled life. Amen."

MORE FROM GOD'S WORD

Romans 11:36
"For of him, and through him, and to him, are all things: to whom be glory for ever. Amen."

2 Timothy 4:18
"And the Lord shall deliver me from every evil work, and will preserve me unto his heavenly kingdom: to whom be glory for ever and ever. Amen."

2 Peter 1:2
"Grace and peace be multiplied unto you through the knowledge of God, and of Jesus our Lord,"

Grow in the root of all grace, which is faith. Believe God's promises more firmly than ever. Allow your faith to increase in its fullness, firmness, and simplicity.
- Charles Spurgeon

5 Minute Journaling

ONE THING I WANT TO REMEMBER ABOUT TODAY'S DEVOTION

_____

_____

_____

_____

_____

TODAY I UNDERSTOOD…

_____

_____

_____

_____

TODAY I'M GRATEFUL FOR…

_____

_____

_____

_____

_____

He Has Your Back

But I trusted in thee, O Lᴏʀᴅ: I said, Thou art my God.
My times are in thy hand: deliver me from the hand of
mine enemies, and from them that persecute me.
Psalms 31:14–15

FOCUS FOR TODAY

God is with us any season we are in.

Bible question for the day. "Whose idea was it that Moses should delegate his responsibilities as a leader of Israel"?

Mountain climbers always travel in groups of at least two to help each other scale the peak before them. The relationship between climbing partners is naturally incredible trust, commitment, and communication. Similarly, soldiers in battle must depend on one another in ways that entrust their safety, and very lives to one another's care. They not only have a responsibility to keep going toward their goal for themselves; they must work as part of a team or partnership.

God is committed to this kind of partnership with us and then some. He wants us to rely on Him in all areas of our lives. He always has our back! While we may face adversity for a reason or our enemies may triumph temporarily, the Lord will consistently deliver us. Like a mother bear protecting her cubs, God loves us with unfailing devotion.

Our soul is for the benefit of humankind; that will last forever!!!

1. Our body. We spend most of our time looking good, but it will leave us when we die.
2. Our wealth and status. For achieving those, we run after the entire life without giving quality time to family and friends. It will go after our death.
3. Our relatives, family, and friends. They will also stay by us up to the graveyard.
4. Our soul. The spiritual or immaterial part of a human being is immortal. We all ignore it due to this world's urging body, wealth, status, and happiness. The soul is the only thing that will last with us forever. We should focus most is on our soul. Souls are essential parts of human beings." All the work we put in sculpting our body came from a desire in our soul. The body without the spirit is dead!!! Only through the grace of God will we get to heaven. Our soul is eternal; we decide one of two places. Heaven or hell? Choose Jesus today. He is in heaven.

The answer to today's Bible question is. "Jethro".

Prayer: "Lord, I'm so glad I can count on You today. You know what I'm going through better than anyone, and I know You're committed to seeing me through it. Lord, thank you for being with me any season I'm in. Help me finish well, Lord, and hold my hands when I'm about drift in this walk. Amen."

MORE FROM GOD'S WORD

Deuteronomy 31:8
"And the Lord, he it is that doth go before thee; he will be with thee, he will not fail thee, neither forsake thee: fear not, neither be dismayed."

Joshua 1:5
"There shall not any man be able to stand before thee all the days of thy life: as I was with Moses, so I will be with thee: I will not fail thee, nor forsake thee."

Psalm 94:14
"For the Lord will not cast off his people, neither will he forsake his inheritance."

"Be encouraged. Hold your head up high and know God is in control and has a plan for you. Instead of focusing on all the bad, be thankful for all the good."
- Germany Kent

5 Minute Journaling

ONE THING I WANT TO REMEMBER ABOUT TODAY'S DEVOTION

_____

_____

_____

_____

_____

TODAY I UNDERSTOOD...

_____

_____

_____

_____

TODAY I'M GRATEFUL FOR...

_____

_____

_____

_____

_____

He Holds Us Firm

The steps of a good man are ordered by the Lord: and he delighteth in his way.
Psalms 37:23

FOCUS FOR TODAY

God is within us wherever we go as we continue
to yield Him moment by moment.

Bible question for the day. "Who recognized Jesus as the Messiah when He was presented at the temple as a baby?"

One of the most significant challenges during lousy weather is maintaining your footing. Whether it's a rainstorm turning the ground to a sloppy mode or freezing snow that leaves the ground icy and treacherous, you have to take each step slowly if you don't want to fall and hurt yourself.

Each year, thousands of people slip and fall regardless of the season, especially in fall and winter. From sprained ankles to broken hips, such injuries leave strong individuals lying on the ground. Even though life circumstances often make us feel as though we are trying to run uphill on a slippery floor, we know that God holds us firm. We only have to take one step at a time, trusting that He guards each one, providing a firm foundation. We may fall occasionally, but our Father always lifts us and helps us get back on our feet. He leads us down a safe path on solid ground. Even with the weather is treacherous and the road seems slick, we can step out in faith and follow Him.

Today, remember that God will never leave you nor forsake you. God loves you. You are not alone; you are an exceptional and divine creation. God desires you will live a life directed with Him that leads to abundance and righteousness. Seek Him today.

The answer to today's Bible question is. "Simeon."

Prayer: "Lord, I look ahead and get afraid sometimes. I don't see a way through the obstacles ahead. Help me to remember to follow you and to take the next step. I trust you, Lord, the things you prepared for me and the right timing. Amen"

MORE FROM GOD'S WORD

John 16:13
"Howbeit when he, the Spirit of truth, is come, he will guide you into all truth: for he shall not speak of himself; but whatsoever he shall hear, that shall he speak: and he will shew you things to come."

Psalm 5:8
"Lead me, O Lᴏʀᴅ, in thy righteousness because of mine enemies; make thy way straight before my face."

Psalm 119:105
"Thy word is a lamp unto my feet, and a light unto my path."

"When you realize God's purpose for your life isn't just about you, He will use you in a mighty way."
- Dr. Tony Evans

5 Minute Journaling

ONE THING I WANT TO REMEMBER ABOUT TODAY'S DEVOTION

_____

_____

_____

_____

_____

TODAY I UNDERSTOOD...

_____

_____

_____

_____

TODAY I'M GRATEFUL FOR...

_____

_____

_____

_____

He Is With US

**The steps of a good man are ordered by the
Lᴏʀᴅ: and he delighteth in his way.
Psalms 37:23**

FOCUS FOR TODAY

If we stumble, the Lord is there to rescue us.

Bible question for the day. "Who recognized Jesus as the Messiah when He was presented at the temple as a baby?"

Often, you are faced with many decisions at the beginning of a new year, you are faced with many decisions. Whether it's scheduling meetings, trips, and events or choosing how you will spend your time and money, you cast a vision for how you'd like the next 12 months to go. You can plan all you want; if the Lord isn't the compass at the heart of your choices, you're bound to get lost. .

When we turn to God and ask for His guidance, He delights in leading us to fulfill our purpose. We may still face obstacles and challenges, but we can preserve knowing that He leads the way before us. Even when suffering painful circumstances, we can experience joy because we know that God is with us, Directing our paths and protecting our hearts.

This passage reminded us about Godly wisdom and having a reverent heart to the Father. If we reject God and His ways, we have consequences here on our earth and our life on eternity. Today, it's a gift that God gives us, the heart of repentance. Whatever we are struggling with and sinning today, we can confess it to the Father and lay at His feet. He is willing to forgive you with our unrighteousness. If we stumble, the Lord is there to rescue us.

The answer to today's Bible question is. "Elizabeth."

Prayer: "Father, reveal the path of life You have for me. Allow me to spend more time with You and listen to Your Spirit. Guide me into becoming the person. You want me to be. Thank you, Lord, for being my rescuer. Amen."

MORE FROM GOD'S WORD

Psalm 37:24
"Though he fall, he shall not be utterly cast down: for the Lord upholdeth him with his hand."

Psalm 40:2
"He brought me up also out of an horrible pit, out of the miry clay, and set my feet upon a rock, and established my goings."

Proverbs 3:1-2
"My son, forget not my law; but let thine heart keep my commandments: 2 For length of days, and long life, and peace, shall they add to thee."

"God doesn't have visiting hours, neither does he sleep. He's there whenever we need him."
- Sarah Christmyer

5 Minute Journaling

ONE THING I WANT TO REMEMBER ABOUT TODAY'S DEVOTION

_____

_____

_____

_____

_____

TODAY I UNDERSTOOD...

_____

_____

_____

_____

TODAY I'M GRATEFUL FOR...

_____

_____

_____

_____

He Knows Your Voice

And thine ears shall hear a word behind thee, saying, This is the way, walk ye in it, when ye turn to the right hand, and when ye turn to the left.
Isaiah 30:21

FOCUS FOR TODAY

God hears our pleas, and He deeply cares for us.

Bible question for the day. "Who witnessed Elijah being taken up to heaven"?

New parents are often amazed at how their hearing suddenly becomes acutely attuned to their newborn's prize. Whether whimpering in their sleep or crying in the church nursery, a baby's attention-getting cry is distinct from any other sound a mother or father may hear. Even among other crying children or in a noisy surrounding, apparent zeros in on their little one's distinct sound. Similarly, babies and children know the voices of their Mother and Father. Many expectant parents were even reading and saying to their baby in the womb, so the newborn will already be familiar with the mom and dad's voices. Sometimes when in distress, a child only needs to recognize the voice of assurance coming from their caretakers.

We, too, as children of God, need to hear our Father's voice and be reassured of His love, guidance, and protection. How wonderful that we can know that He hears us as well – distinct and unique from all His other sons and daughters!

Stay in the moment; the last moment is gone; the next moment is not here yet; continuously tell yourself in your mind, right at this very moment, everything is okay. Fear knocked, Faith answered, no one was there. Faith believes in something far more significant than ourselves; you cannot see. If you know you have a heart, soul, mind, and spirit, these are things we cannot see. We cannot see gravity, wind, the heat of the sun, and atoms; there are more things unseen than there are things seen. And only God knows our heart. Today, whatever you feel, take comfort that He sees and hears your voice. Seek Him first. Cry out to Him.

The answer to today's Bible question is. "Elisha."

Prayer: "Abba Father, thank you for listening when I cry out for Your help. I am so glad that You hear my prayers and come to my aid. Thank you, Lord, for rescuing me in the moments of despair and helplessness. Give me strength and courage to press on daily. Amen."

MORE FROM GOD'S WORD

Isaiah 26:20
"Come, my people, enter thou into thy chambers, and shut thy doors about thee: hide thyself as it were for a little moment, until the indignation be overpast."

Psalm 56:8-9
"8 Thou tellest my wanderings: put thou my tears into thy bottle: are they not in thy book? 9 When I cry unto thee, then shall mine enemies turn back: this I know; for God is for me."

Psalms 121:1-2
"1 I will lift up mine eyes unto the hills, from whence cometh my help. 2 My help cometh from the LORD, which made heaven and earth."

Sometimes the greatest worship comes from a broken heart. Sometimes praise comes from tears. Sometimes all we need to do is hand our burdens to Christ as our offering. We don't have to pretend to God. He can handle our sorrow, struggles. He is not judging or saying you are too much. He treasures your tears just as much as your praise.
- Rachel Hamilton

5 Minute Journaling

ONE THING I WANT TO REMEMBER ABOUT TODAY'S DEVOTION

_____

_____

_____

_____

_____

TODAY I UNDERSTOOD…

_____

_____

_____

_____

TODAY I'M GRATEFUL FOR…

_____

_____

_____

_____

He Remains The Same

Thy kingdom is an everlasting kingdom, and thy dominion endureth throughout all generations.
Psalm 145:13

FOCUS FOR TODAY

We can depend on God's promises in this
broken world. Hold on to Him alone.

Bible question for the day. Which comes first, "The book of Nehemiah or Esther?""?

Even though weather can be unpredictable and changeable quickly, the four seasons remain constant. Some days may seem like they include all four and one by starting cool, growing warmer, blowing in a storm, revealing the sun, clouding up and turning chilly again, and ending with a few snowflakes. Depending on where you live, this may be more the norm than not. However, over time, there are still characteristics of each season that remain constant. In summer, on average, the temperatures are higher. In winter, colder weather lingers more regularly. We learn that even though a particular day may be exceptional, the seasons on average remain constant.

With each day's variant conditions, if the seasons remain consistent, we can trust that God's faithfulness remains the same regardless of our life circumstances. God's promises are true. What has the Lord been speaking to you lately? Trust to His word and promises. His promises are what we can depend upon in this broken world. He is the same yesterday, today, and forever! May the Lord encourage you today. Don't give up. Hold on to His promises.

The answer to today's Bible question is. "The book of Nehemiah comes first."

Prayer: "Dear God, even though my circumstances change and seem to go up and down, I'm grateful that You're always there, my solid rock. Thank you, Lord, for giving me the promises that I can hold on to. Speak to me, Lord, and allow my heart to hear and receive your truth. I surrender my life to you, Lord. Amen."

MORE FROM GOD'S WORD

1 Timothy 1:17
"Now unto the King eternal, immortal, invisible, the only wise God, be honour and glory for ever and ever. Amen."

2 Peter 1:11
"For so an entrance shall be ministered unto you abundantly into the everlasting kingdom of our Lord and Saviour Jesus Christ."

Psalm 10:16
*"The L*ORD* is King for ever and ever: the heathen are perished out of his land."*

"Hold fast to your faith.
Keep your hope in the Lord. Embrace the love of God."
- Lailah Gifty Akita, T

"The best praying man is the man who is most believingly familiar with the promises of God. After all, prayer is nothing but taking God's promises to him, and saying to him, "Do as thou hast said." Prayer is the promise utilized. A prayer which is not based on a promise has no true foundation."
- Charles Spurgeon,

5 Minute Journaling

ONE THING I WANT TO REMEMBER ABOUT TODAY'S DEVOTION

_____

_____

_____

_____

_____

TODAY I UNDERSTOOD…

_____

_____

_____

_____

TODAY I'M GRATEFUL FOR…

_____

_____

_____

_____

He Sees

And she called the name of the LORD **that spake unto her, Thou God seest me: for she said, Have I also here looked after him that seeth me?**
Genesis 16:13

FOCUS FOR TODAY

God sees you. He deeply cares about you. You are not alone.

Bible question for the day. "Who stopped Abraham from slaying his son"?

You stand and look out your window, and you may see traffic or trees or other houses or people, and the thought runs through your mind. No one knows what my life is like. No one knows what goes on inside me. You feel alone. If you entertain the thought, self-pity elbows itself in – and no one cares. Even if you have close relationships with friends and family, sometimes in moments of quiet, of solitude, we can feel isolated in the world. And the truth is, we are.

We were created by God and for God, in His image. That means that only God can reach places inside of us. As good as life can be at times, there is nowhere as good as closeness to God because God knows us. God knows all about it. God knows that sometimes you do not enjoy being with your children. God knows that the special people in your life do not always "get" you. God knows that you may not talk to anyone some days and you feel forgotten. God sees you. And God loves you.

In the darkest moments and despair, we have El Roi, the God Who sees. In our lowest moments, God sees our pain. He is with us. He hears the cries we have that no one sees. There may be no fix quick for our problems, yet God sees the bigger perspective of our problem in eternal thoughts. We can be lonely with people, but once we have God, we are never lonely, even we are alone. Don't give up. He sees with you today.

The answer to today's Bible question is. "The angel of the Lord."

Prayer: "Jesus, thank you for you will never leave me and that you care deeply about the things that concern me. Please help me to sense your presence as I go through my day. Thank you, Lord, that you know me individually and deeply see me. Lord, I pray for growth and healing in my life as I continue to fix my eyes in you alone. Amen."

MORE FROM GOD'S WORD

Psalm 56:8
"Thou tellest my wanderings: put thou my tears into thy bottle: are they not in thy book?"

Proverbs 15:3
"The eyes of the LORD are in every place, beholding the evil and the good."

Psalm 33:18
"Behold, the eye of the LORD is upon them that fear him, upon them that hope in his mercy;"

Your work may not be noticed by people, but there is One Who sees everything you are doing.
- Sunday Adelaja

God sees nothing but beauty in you.
- Kate Wicker

5 Minute Journaling

ONE THING I WANT TO REMEMBER ABOUT TODAY'S DEVOTION

_____
_____
_____
_____
_____

TODAY I UNDERSTOOD…

_____
_____
_____
_____

TODAY I'M GRATEFUL FOR…

_____
_____
_____
_____

He Will Guide US

For this God is our God for ever and ever: he will be our guide even unto death.
Psalm 48:14

FOCUS FOR TODAY

God constantly provides us His guidance and direction. Seek Him today.

Bible question for the day. "What is the truth?"

We don't have to worry much about directions anymore. We have many gadgets, apps, and programs to help us navigate our destinations. Most of them get us there by the most direct route possible, occasionally factoring in variables such as traffic, construction, and weather. Sometimes, though, mapping systems aren't up to date or contain a glitch that sends us on a tangent or, worse, gets us lost.

Similarly, our lives seem to take the direct route from one milestone to another. At the same time, we might like the predictable that comes from knowing exactly where we are going and how we will get there; much of the time, we don't. This doesn't mean we don't have a reliable guide, however. God constantly provides us with His guidance and direction. When we trust Him with each decision we make and each step we take, we can rest in His sovereignty.

The answer to today's Bible question is, "Pontius Pilate asked Jesus that question, "what is the truth."

John 5:27-38

And he has given Him authority to judge because He is the Son of Man. "Do not be amazed at this, for a time is coming when all who are in their graves will hear HIs voice 29 and come out—those who have done what is good will rise to live, and those who have done what is evil will rise to be condemned. 30 By myself I can do nothing; I judge only as I hear, and my judgment is just, for I seek not to please myself but him who sent me. "If I testify about myself, my testimony is not true. 32 There is another who testifies in my favor, and I know that his testimony about me is true. "You have sent to John and he has testified to the truth. 34 Not that I accept human testimony; but I mention it that you may be saved. 35 John was a lamp that burned and gave light, and you chose for a time to enjoy his light. "I have testimony weightier than that of John. For the works that the Father has given me to finish—the very works that I am doing—testify that the Father has sent me. 37 And the Father who sent me has himself testified concerning me. You have never heard his voice nor seen his form, 38 nor does his word dwell in you, for you do not believe the one he sent.

Prayer: "Father, even though I don't know all that's about to happen today, I know that You do. Guide me each step of the way, leaving me to the center of where You want me. I entrust to you my life, Lord.

MORE FROM GOD'S WORD

Psalm 32:8
"I will instruct you and teach you in the way you should go; I will counsel you with my eye upon you".

Psalm 37:23-24
"23 The steps of a good man are ordered by the LORD: and he delighteth in his way 24 Though he fall, he shall not be utterly cast down: for the LORD upholdeth him with his hand.

Psalm 118
"O give thanks unto the LORD; for he is good: because his mercy endureth for ever."

"Earthly wisdom is doing what comes naturally. Godly wisdom is doing what the Holy Spirit compels us to do."
- Charles Stanley

"The place God calls you to is the place where your deep gladness and the world's deep hunger meet."
- Frederick Buechner

5 Minute Journaling

ONE THING I WANT TO REMEMBER ABOUT TODAY'S DEVOTION

_____

_____

_____

_____

_____

TODAY I UNDERSTOOD...

_____

_____

_____

_____

_____

TODAY I'M GRATEFUL FOR...

_____

_____

_____

_____

_____

Healing Our Hurts

The LORD is nigh unto them that are of a broken
heart; and saveth such as be of a contrite spirit.
Psalms 34:18

FOCUS FOR TODAY

God has a purpose for your pain. He is with you!

Bible question for the day. "In Daniel's dream, how many beasts emerged from the sea?"

When we were children, it only took a moment in our parents' arms to get over a scraped knee or spilled cup of juice. The sense of closeness provided a tangible comfort to our distress. We felt safe and secure, aware that our painful problem bothered us but that our mother's or father's loving presence was more significant than any problem we encountered.

As we grow up, we learn to handle our painful losses and disappointments by ourselves - to tough it out and push through. But often, these injuries never heal. They linger only to ache even more acutely. We still need our Father's embrace when we stumble and fall. Whether it is a day where nothing goes right for a significant life loss, we must remember that someone is more prominent than even the most essential obstacle we may face. This verse reminded us that God fully understands us and our hurts. God watches and hears the cry of the righteous. He protects and redeems us. Even when we feel broken and crushed, God comforts us with His care. Today, If you are in a season of overwhelming challenges, pains, tribulations. Don't give up. God is with you! May God give you the courage to breathe again.

The answer to today's Bible question is "four beasts."

Prayer: "Remind me, Father, that You are always there for me, willing to comfort me." And put my heart back together whenever it breaks. I pray for myself currently feeling weak, brokenhearted, lost, lonely, or alone. I pray that I will find my strength and purpose in You. Guide them through this day and renew my hope and strength. Amen."

MORE FROM GOD'S WORD

3 John 1:2
"Beloved, I wish above all things that thou mayest prosper and be in health, even as thy soul prospereth."

Revelation 21:4
"And God shall wipe away all tears from their eyes; and there shall be no more death, neither sorrow, nor crying, neither shall there be any more pain: for the former things are passed away."

2 Kings 20:5
"Turn again, and tell Hezekiah the captain of my people, Thus saith the LORD, the God of David thy father, I have heard thy prayer, I have seen thy tears: behold, I will heal thee: on the third day thou shalt go up unto the house of the LORD.'"

Leave the broken, irreversible past in God's hands, and step out into the invincible future with Him.
- Oswald Chambers

5 Minute Journaling

ONE THING I WANT TO REMEMBER ABOUT TODAY'S DEVOTION

_____

_____

_____

_____

_____

TODAY I UNDERSTOOD…

_____

_____

_____

_____

TODAY I'M GRATEFUL FOR…

_____

_____

_____

_____

His Holy Promise

For he remembered his holy promise, and Abraham his servant.
Psalm 105:42

FOCUS FOR TODAY

God doesn't withhold good gifts to us, which
is salvation that came from Him alone.

Bible question for the day. "The French word "Noel" is often used around Christmas, but what was its original meaning in Latin"?

At Christmas, we celebrate the birth of Jesus in many ways. Among them, we incorporate family traditions and bring out heirloom ornaments and unique decorations. Many of these traditions and items have been passed down from generation to generation, all the more remarkable as we realize that our parents' grandparents enjoyed the same unique elements of their Christmas celebration. Just as we want the individual family elements handed down at Christmas, we are reminded of our eternal inheritance. God promised His people that He would make a way to save them from their disobedience and bad choices. He promised to send them a Savior, His Son, Christ our Lord.

Our Father always keeps His promises, and the greatest one of all remains our most precious gift, a Baby in a manger wrapped in swaddling clothes.

God loves you. God is proud of you. Stay in the moment; at this very moment, everything will be okay.

The answer to today's Bible question is, "The Latin word for "Noel" means, "birth."

Prayer: "Today, Lord, I want to prepare my heart to celebrate Your birth. Thank you for Your sacrifice, for the gift of salvation, and eternal life. I am heartily sorry for ever having offended thee, I detest all my sins because of thy just punishment, but most of all because they have offended thee my God, who art all good and deserving of all my love, I firmly resolve with the help of thy grace, to sin no more and avoid the near occasions of sin. Amen"

5 Minute Journaling

ONE THING I WANT TO REMEMBER ABOUT TODAY'S DEVOTION

TODAY I UNDERSTOOD...

TODAY I'M GRATEFUL FOR...

MORE FROM GOD'S WORD

Psalm 145:9
"The Lord is good to all: and his tender mercies are over all his works."

1 Chronicles 16:34
"O give thanks unto the Lord; for he is good; for his mercy endureth for ever."

Psalm 100:5
"For the Lord is good; his mercy is everlasting; and his truth endureth to all generations."

"Faith is a process whereby you hold on to God's promises because you know that he will fulfil each one of them."
- Gift Gugu Mona

5 Minute Journaling

ONE THING I WANT TO REMEMBER ABOUT TODAY'S DEVOTION

_____

_____

_____

_____

_____

TODAY I UNDERSTOOD…

_____

_____

_____

_____

TODAY I'M GRATEFUL FOR…

_____

_____

_____

_____

His Indescribable Gift

Thanks be unto God for his unspeakable gift.
2 Corinthians 9:15

FOCUS FOR TODAY

God's greatest gift is Jesus.

Bible question for the day. "How many days after the birth of Christ did Joseph and Mary give Him the name Jesus?

What are the best gifts you've ever received at Christmas throughout your entire lifetime? Did you get a pony when you were growing up? A new bicycle that you dreamed about? A favorite doll, drum set, or iPod? Or maybe you've been blessed to receive some presents as an adult that left you speechless; perhaps an engagement ring, a new car, a precious family heirloom, or a surprise vacation.

Regardless of your best gifts, none of them can compare with the ultimate gift – the incredible gift of grace and eternal life! God gave us His most precious, most beloved Son, knowing that this time on earth would not be easy. And yet, our Father knew that this was the only gift that could bridge the gap between our sins and His Holiness. It's always memorable to give and receive larger-than-life, breath-taking gifts. But the most dazzling gift of all has already been given. Today, whatever struggles you face, remember that all of these things we experience are done and paid on the cross. This world isn't our final home; this is not our final destination.

God's love is so vast and beyond our wisdom, knowledge, comprehension, or imagination. God's love is also equal to God's wrath. The depths of hell and the feeling of evil for an eternal destination are beyond our wisdom, knowledge, comprehension, or imagination. A blink of an eye is 14,000s a second. Our life here on this earth is less than that compared to eternity. God's gift to us is life; our gift to God is what we do with this life. Enjoy God's gift of living with Jesus today.

The answer to today's Bible question is, "Eight days after Jesus Christ our Lord's birth."

Prayer: "Jesus, You gave Your life for me. I want to give my life for You. Mold me, Lord. Amen."

MORE FROM GOD'S WORD

John 3:16
"For God so loved the world, that he gave his only begotten Son, that whosoever believeth in him should not perish, but have everlasting life.".

Romans 8:18
"For I reckon that the sufferings of this present time are not worthy to be compared with the glory which shall be revealed in us."

1 Peter 4:10
"As every man hath received the gift, even so minister the same one to another, as good stewards of the manifold grace of God."

"God, you love me so much that you gave your one and only Son for me. Because I believe in Jesus, I will not perish, but have eternal life."
- Nancy DeJesus

5 Minute Journaling

ONE THING I WANT TO REMEMBER ABOUT TODAY'S DEVOTION

_____

_____

_____

_____

_____

TODAY I UNDERSTOOD...

_____

_____

_____

_____

TODAY I'M GRATEFUL FOR...

_____

_____

_____

_____

His Love Remains

The LORD is longsuffering, and of great mercy, forgiving iniquity and transgression, and by no means clearing the guilty, visiting the iniquity of the fathers upon the children unto the third and fourth generation.
Numbers 14:18

FOCUS FOR TODAY

God is gracious and ready to forgive our trespasses. Come back to Him.

Bible question for the day. Who were the parents of Cain and Abel"?

We handle each anger differently. Some people snap back immediately when something sets them off and makes their anger part of their default defensive setting. Others may go weeks or even months before they reach their boiling point. Some people express their anger through words, while others take – or avoid taking – action to communicate their displeasure.

With God, we are told He is slow to anger. And even when we disappoint Him through our disobedience, His love for us leads to His forgiveness when we confess our sins to Him. He doesn't blow up like a hot-head with a short fuse. We don't have to walk on eggshells out of fear that He will explode with rage. Greater still, we know that even when God is angry, His love and compassion remain. He will not become so furious with us that He cannot forgive us. His nature is love, and through the gift of His Son, Jesus, He's always chosen to ignore us so that we can be with Him forever.

God does not make junk, and God does not make mistakes. You are a divine creation and a child of God. With unshakable faith, do not worry. Do not stress those moments of confidence and happiness you will not get back anymore, and that's what the devil would like you to do: stress and worry, and the people, places, and things rent space in your head. Keep the happiness, the joy, the peace, and the love for God through Jesus Christ our Lord and pray to God and thank Him for this day, praising the Lord and praying to show love for God at least once a day or twice a day when you wake up in the morning say, "thank you, God." When you go to bed at night, say, "thank you for this day, God." No matter what happens, His love remains. Thank Him, always!

The answer to today's Bible question is, "Adam and Eve."

Prayer: "Lord, I'm grateful that You are slow to anger and don't express Your anger the way people do. Help me control my anger and show mercy to those who provoke me. Lord, remove the junk in my heart and allow me to release forgiveness to the people who hurt me. Amen."

MORE FROM GOD'S WORD

Proverbs 15:1
"A soft answer turneth away wrath: but grievous words stir up anger."

Proverbs 15:18
"A wrathful man stirreth up strife: but he that is slow to anger appeaseth strife."

Psalm 103:8
"The Lord is merciful and gracious, slow to anger, and plenteous in mercy."

The anger of God proceeds with a slow step to avenge itself, but that it compensates for its tardiness by the severity of its punishment.
- John Calvin

5 Minute Journaling

ONE THING I WANT TO REMEMBER ABOUT TODAY'S DEVOTION

_____

_____

_____

_____

_____

TODAY I UNDERSTOOD...

_____

_____

_____

_____

TODAY I'M GRATEFUL FOR...

_____

_____

_____

_____

His Way

For my thoughts are not your thoughts, neither
are your ways my ways, saith the Lord.
Isaiah 55:8

FOCUS FOR TODAY

God's ways and will are higher than ours. Trust Him today.

Bible question for the day. "Which woman tried to kill Elijah after he put the prophets of Baal to death?"

Part of what we appreciate about other people and what often frustrates us is our differences. When a problem emerges in a group, each member might solve it uniquely. One person might address the problem head-on, while another might wait as long as possible to see what develops. One individual would break the problem into small components that take time to address, while another looks for the quickest solution to the most significant issue. Most of us think that we know how specific problems in our lives should be fixed. If only we believe, or why can't they see what must be done? We come up with ways that events could proceed to get what we want when we want it. This rarely happens, however.

While God wants us to be actively engaged with life, He also wants us to depend on Him. Our way of doing things – especially when it comes to problem-solving – is not the same as His way. His perspective cuts across time, geography, history, culture, and other barriers that can cloud our perspective. Our Father truly knows best.

We need to remember Who God is more than our life and circumstances with unshakable faith. We may feel disappointed, crushed, or hopeless, but we need to focus on God alone. We trust His ways and will.

The answer to today's Bible question is. "Jezebel."

Prayer: Lord, I'm glad that You empowered me to solve problems. But help me see your perspective on when, how, and why things happen. Amen."

MORE FROM GOD'S WORD

Philippians 4; 4 – 5
"4 Rejoice in the Lord always: and again I say, Rejoice. 5 Let your moderation be known unto all men. The Lord is at hand."

Romans 11:33
"O the depth of the riches both of the wisdom and knowledge of God! how unsearchable are his judgments, and his ways past finding out!"

Psalm 86:11
"Teach me thy way, O Lᴏʀᴅ; I will walk in thy truth: unite my heart to fear thy name."

"I'm reminded that, often, God allows us to wrestle for long periods of time as we reach out for Him."
- Henry Cloud

5 Minute Journaling

ONE THING I WANT TO REMEMBER ABOUT TODAY'S DEVOTION

_____

_____

_____

_____

_____

TODAY I UNDERSTOOD…

_____

_____

_____

_____

_____

TODAY I'M GRATEFUL FOR…

_____

_____

_____

_____

_____

Laugh Regularly

A merry heart doeth good like a medicine:
but a broken spirit drieth the bones.
Proverbs 17:22

FOCUS FOR TODAY

To be able to laugh even in distress is a grace. Pray for it.

Bible question for the day. The Bible question for the day. "What is the eighth commandment

When was the last time you laughed until tears streamed down your face? Maybe it was watching a funny movie with family, sharing a joke with coworkers, or cracking up or one of your own mistakes. Regardless of what led you to laugh, we see that laughter is good medicine for souls in God's word. When we can lighten our load by seeing a different perspective or celebrating the silliness in an unexpected situation, we are often reminded of our limitations and God's power and sovereignty.

Sometimes we become so burdened by the weight of all we carry. Pressured by the demands of our many responsibilities, we forget to laugh. Our heart becomes hardened, and our joy dries up by laughing regularly and frequently restores a wellspring of joy and gratitude in our lives. We pause and realize that we do not have to be responsible for every detail today. God is in control.

Do you have to put a coat hanger in your mouth at night to wake up with a smile on your face? Do you feel if you smiled, your face would crack and fall off? Try it sometime. It could very well be the answer to someone's prayer. You don't have to be a mental midget all of your life. Smile. God loves to see you enjoying the gift of life.

The answer to today's Bible question is. "Exodus 20; 16. – Thou shalt not bear false witness against thy neighbor."

Prayer: Father, don't let me become so serious that I lose the ability to laugh. Thank You for giving me a sense of humor and the joyful medicine it works on my soul. Give me a spirit and heart that see the good in every situation. Heal me, Lord, and give me the joy I need today. Amen."

MORE FROM GOD'S WORD

Psalm 34:18
*"The L*ORD *is nigh unto them that are of a broken heart; and saveth such as be of a contrite spirit."*

Ecclesiastes 3:4
"A time to weep, and a time to laugh; a time to mourn, and a time to dance;"

Ecclesiastes 10:19
"A feast is made for laughter, and wine maketh merry: but money answereth all things."

No man in the world should be so happy as a man of God. It is one continual source of gladness. He can look up and say, "God is my Father, Christ is my Saviour, and the Church is my mother."
- Dwight L. Moody

5 Minute Journaling

ONE THING I WANT TO REMEMBER ABOUT TODAY'S DEVOTION

_____
_____
_____
_____
_____

TODAY I UNDERSTOOD…

_____
_____
_____
_____

TODAY I'M GRATEFUL FOR…

_____
_____
_____
_____

Let It Snow

**Purge me with hyssop, and I shall be clean: wash me, and I shall be whiter than snow. Make me to hear joy and gladness; that the bones which thou hast broken may rejoice. Hide thy face from my sins, and blot out all mine iniquities.
Psalm 51:7-9**

FOCUS FOR TODAY

God is willing to forgive us. He is there
waiting for us. Come back to Him.

Bible question for the day. "What killed the apostle Matthew"?

Unless you live in high mountains or the southern hemisphere, you're probably not accustomed to seeing snow in June. Snow is packed with frozen iced crystals. When seeing snow represents beauty, purity, and holiness. No matter how dirty we seem, we are, just as like snow, God is there to forgive us. When we confess our sins before the Lord and ask for His forgiveness, we can know the clean, white freshens of snowfall within our hearts all year round. When we harbor sin in our lives, we begin to feel weary, dirty, and burdened by the weight of our selfishness. Left to our own devices, we can try to make amends, read self-improvement books, and justify our mistakes. But only God can forgive us and make us new again. Only He can watch us clean and make us feel as beautiful as a muddy field blanketed by snow looks. Spent some time confessing your sins before the Lord, asking Him to let it snow in your heart.

God loves you; you are a divine creation; there has never been one of you, and there will never be another. Keep that smile on your face and the joy of the Holy Spirit within you continuously being happy, joyous, and free, not letting people, places, or things rent space in your head. It is only room for you and God and the Holy Spirit working through you to help others. God loves you and waiting for you to repent on Him. Be brave.

The answer to today's Bible question is "A halberd (a combined spear-ax)

Prayer: "Lord, thank You for forgiving my sins when I confess them before You. I confess, Lord, that I am a sinner, and I need your grace and strength daily. Help me resist any forms of temptation and deliver me from any wickedness of this world. Thank You for washing me white as snow. Thank you, Father, for your grace and mercy. I want to honor you in my life. Amen."

MORE FROM GOD'S WORD

Proverbs 28:13
"He that covereth his sins shall not prosper: but whoso confesseth and forsaketh them shall have mercy."

Leviticus 5:5
"And it shall be, when he shall be guilty in one of these things, that he shall confess that he hath sinned in that thing:"

Acts 3:19
"Repent ye therefore, and be converted, that your sins may be blotted out, when the times of refreshing shall come from the presence of the Lord."

It is not the healthy who need a doctor, but the sick. I have not come to call the righteous, but sinners to repentance. Jesus Christ

Forgiveness is always free. But that doesn't mean that confession is always easy. Sometimes it is hard. Incredibly hard. It is painful to admit our sins and entrust ourselves to God's care.
- Erwin Lutzer

5 Minute Journaling

ONE THING I WANT TO REMEMBER ABOUT TODAY'S DEVOTION

_____

_____

_____

_____

_____

TODAY I UNDERSTOOD...

_____

_____

_____

_____

TODAY I'M GRATEFUL FOR...

_____

_____

_____

_____

Lionhearted

**The wicked flee when no man pursueth: but
the righteous are bold as a lion.
Proverbs 28:1**

FOCUS FOR TODAY

You can rely on God to empower and give you the
courage you need today. Be courageous.

Bible question for the day. "Which gospel records the fewest of the miracles performed by Jesus"?

As Christians, we sometimes feel we should be made mild, nice and quiet, reserved, and even passive in interacting with others around us. However, nothing could be further from the truth! Jesus tells us to be the salt and light, flavor and illumination to the bland darkness of the world. We are said to be bold in how we love others, letting our light shine rather than hiding it away. Even if you do not think of your- self as a bull person, you can rely on God to empower you and give you the courage to take action. With nothing to fear, you can proceed with the same fears, determination, and confidence strength as a king of the beasts. Christ was called the lion of Judah, and like Him, we can move with calm authority through our day.

Today, be a lion in the way you pursue loving others, fierce and deter-mined, regal and majestic. No resentments, no regrets we cannot turn the clock backward, continue to move forward growing along spiritual lines trying to help those lost to meet Jesus in heaven. Because we are Christians, we have the courage, and we are courageous; we are not doormats that should be walked on. Wake up and smell the thorns; when the going gets tough, the tough get going. Fear knocked, Faith answered, and nobody was there. God's gift to us is life; what we do with this life is our gift to God. And it is not living in the rearview mirror, letting others intimidate you, or using you as a doormat. Spun the devil around and bid him farewell and never look back. Don't let the coward, liar, thief, greedy, and lustful control your life. All liars will go to hell. And those are the gutless cowards that may intimidate the lesser than thou, but not God's children. The only thing we fear is God.

John 14; 8. – If God is all you have, you have all you need.

The answer to today's Bible question is. "The Gospel of Matthew."

Prayer: "Dear God, it is not easy for me to be bold about my faith sometimes. Give me the courage, power, and confidence to be like the lion of Judah. Amen".

MORE FROM GOD'S WORD

Joshua 1:7
"Only be thou strong and very courageous, that thou mayest observe to do according to all the law, which Moses my servant commanded thee: turn not from it to the right hand or to the left, that thou mayest prosper withersoever thou goest."

Psalm 31:24
"Be of good courage, and he shall strengthen your heart, all ye that hope in the LORD."

Ephesians 6:10
"Finally, my brethren, be strong in the Lord, and in the power of his might."

You must be bold, brave, and courageous and find a way... to get in the way.
- John Lewis

5 Minute Journaling

ONE THING I WANT TO REMEMBER ABOUT TODAY'S DEVOTION

_____

_____

_____

_____

_____

TODAY I UNDERSTOOD...

_____

_____

_____

_____

TODAY I'M GRATEFUL FOR...

_____

_____

_____

_____

Love Your Neighbor

**Thou shalt not avenge, nor bear any grudge
against the children of thy people, but thou shalt
love thy neighbour as thyself: I am the Lord.
Leviticus 19:18**

FOCUS FOR TODAY

We ought to love our neighbors, even the difficult ones.

Bible question for the day. "When the Lord told Abraham that his wife would have a child, what was his reaction?

Our neighbors are all around us, whether we live next door to them or even know their names. The young woman is serving our coffee, the older gentleman sitting across from us on the bus, the teenager in your youth group at church. Anyone with whom we come in contact is our neighbor. And we are told to treat them – no, to love them – the same way we love and regard ourselves.

A follower of Jesus as Kim, "Lord, who is my neighbor?" And His answer probably surprised and maybe even disturbed them. Christ said that our neighbors are all around us, daily people we encounter. It might be easier to categorize the friendly people next door as the only ones we need to treat with kindness, but that is not what God tells us. Before we can love others is are we ought to also ourselves first. The love we show to them is the love we received and experienced from our Heavenly Father. Loving our neighbors entails forgiving, praying, and blessing them. Today, love every neighbor you encounter, not just those who live close by.

The answer to today's Bible question is.

"Abraham left (Genesis 17; 16 – 17. And I will bless her, and give thee a son also of her; yes, I will bless her, and she shall be a mother of nations; kings of people shall be of her. 17. Then Abraham fell upon his face, and laughed, and said in his heart, shall a child be born unto him that is an hundred years old? And shall Sarah that is 90 years old, bear? They named her son Isaac, and Isaac means laughter in Hebrew.

Prayer: "Lord, help me to love my neighbors as myself, to serve those around me with the selflessness attitude. Amen."

MORE FROM GOD'S WORD

Philippians 2:3
"Let nothing be done through strife or vainglory; but in lowliness of mind let each esteem other better than themselves."

Matthew 6:14-15
"14 For if ye forgive men their trespasses, your heavenly Father will also forgive you: 15 But if ye forgive not men their trespasses, neither will your Father forgive your trespasses."

John 15:13
"Greater love hath no man than this, that a man lay down his life for his friends."

"Love each other dearly always. There is scarcely anything else in the world but that: to love one another."
- Victor Hugo

"To love one another means to have compassionate concern and care for all people. It is to know the value of living a good life, and of adding value to others life. It produces a meaningful life!"
- Joan Jessalyn Cox

5 Minute Journaling

ONE THING I WANT TO REMEMBER ABOUT TODAY'S DEVOTION

_____

_____

_____

_____

_____

TODAY I UNDERSTOOD…

_____

_____

_____

_____

_____

TODAY I'M GRATEFUL FOR…

_____

_____

_____

_____

_____

Mind Control

**For to be carnally minded is death; but to be
spiritually minded is life and peace.
Romans 8:6**

FOCUS FOR TODAY

Allow the Holy Spirit to control your mind today.

Bible question for the day. "By showing hospitality to strangers, who have some entertained unaware?"

When we consider our minds being controlled, it sounds rather ominous, like space aliens or nanochips implanted by spies as part of a government conspiracy. This kind of "mind control" may turn up frequently in science fiction stories and big-screen spy thrillers. However, there is a real sense that what we focus our thinking on will determine what and who controls the landscape of our minds. When we focus on our fears, responsibilities, obligations, and problems, we allow our minds to be controlled by anxiety and worry. When we allow God's Holy Spirit to control our minds, we experience life and peace, not worry and doubt. God has everything under control, and we must trust Him fully – with our body, soul, and mind. Today, consider the way your thoughts shape your expectations and color your perspective.

A father says to his son, "Which one do you love more, me or mommy? The son says, "I love you both." The father then says, "very well, let us say I went to Japan and Mommy went to France, which country will you go to"? The sun then says, "Japan." The father then says, "See, that shows me you love mommy more than me?" The son then says, "no, I just want to visit Japan." The father then says, "very well, let us say I went to Japan and Mommy went to France, which country where you go to?" The son then says, "France." The father then says, "See?" The son says, "no, it's just because I have already visited Japan."

The answer to today's Bible question is. "Angels."

Prayer: "Holy Spirit, you are the only one Whom I want controlling my mind. Remind me of your truth and dispel the fears and worries that try to dominate my thinking. Remove any fears, worries, and anxieties in my mind. I want to live in fullness, joy, and freedom. Help me, Lord, and deliver me. Amen."

MORE FROM GOD'S WORD

Hebrews 13:2
"Be not forgetful to entertain strangers: for thereby some have entertained angels unawares."

Colossians 3:2
"Set your affection on things above, not on things on the earth."

Philippians 4:7
"And the peace of God, which passeth all understanding, shall keep your hearts and minds through Christ Jesus."

"Control your thoughts and everything will be under your control."
- Debasish Mridha

5 Minute Journaling

ONE THING I WANT TO REMEMBER ABOUT TODAY'S DEVOTION

_____

_____

_____

_____

_____

TODAY I UNDERSTOOD…

_____

_____

_____

_____

TODAY I'M GRATEFUL FOR…

_____

_____

_____

_____

Never Ashamed

For I am not ashamed of the gospel of Christ: for it
is the power of God unto salvation to every one that
believeth; to the Jew first, and also to the Greek.
Romans 1:16

FOCUS FOR TODAY

Gospel and the power of Christ enable us to live
a victorious life. Never be ashamed.

Bible question for the day. "For how many years did the children of Israel wander in the wilderness?"

Sometimes no matter how hard we try, we just don't fit into our surroundings. Whether in a crowd of people very different from us or exploring a new culture on vacation, we can't hide our differences. We may feel like the proverbial sore thumb, sticking out as a newcomer, a transfer, or a tourist, apologizing for our additional questions or lack of familiarity with procedure or etiquette.

However, we never have to apologize or feel ashamed for being a follower of Jesus. Sometimes we may cringe when we see other people claiming to know God condemning others, lying about circumstances, or acting hypocritically. Yes, this may create a false impression of believers and other people's minds. All the more reason, we must reflect the goodness, grace, and gentleness of Christ.

Today, make it clear to those around you that you love Jesus – not by what you say but by what you do. No matter what you are going through these days, never be ashamed. Gospel compels all of it and the darkness we are going through. God's power is within us.

The answer to today's Bible question is. "The children of Israel wandered around the desert, for 40 years, because of their constant complaining. And Moses was not to see the promised land because God asked Moses to speak to the rock to bring forth water. Instead, Moses hit the rock with his staff and angry at the complaining children of Israel.

Prayer: "Jesus, I want to be a light in the darkness, drawing others to your love and the gift of salvation. Shine through me so that others see your truth. Amen."

MORE FROM GOD'S WORD

Romans 10:11
"For the scripture saith, Whosoever believeth on him shall not be ashamed."

Isaiah 28:16
"Therefore thus saith the Lord GOD, Behold, I lay in Zion for a foundation a stone, a tried stone, a precious corner stone, a sure foundation: he that believeth shall not make haste."

The glory of the gospel is that when the church is absolutely different from the world, she invariably attracts it.
- Martyn Lloyd-Jones

"You have one business on earth – to save souls."
- John Wesley

5 Minute Journaling

ONE THING I WANT TO REMEMBER ABOUT TODAY'S DEVOTION

_____

_____

_____

_____

_____

TODAY I UNDERSTOOD…

_____

_____

_____

_____

TODAY I'M GRATEFUL FOR…

_____

_____

_____

_____

New Insights

I will instruct thee and teach thee in the way which
thou shalt go: I will guide thee with mine eye.
Psalm 32:8

FOCUS FOR TODAY

God never runs out of teaching and counsel to us. Listen to
Him today.

Bible question for the day. "And what language did Jesus speak?"

Each day provides us with new learning opportunities. We don't have to be in school or training for a new career or experience life lessons. God delights in teaching us His truth. Through His word, we have the opportunity to study His many lessons, each day discovering a new insight or fresh angle to the only certainty that endures forever.

God also reveals His instructions to us through prayer and our relationships with one another. While we may not have the answer we want when we want it, or the wisdom to see that perspective of our Father, we can still know that He will guide us. Like a hiker lost in the woods discovering her compass, we don't have to rely on our knowledge alone.

This verse fills with promise showing the best pathway of our life in our walk with Christ. We are never run out of His sight, even at the pit, crossroads, detours, or dead ends. God will always guide us as we listen to Him daily. Today, notice what God is trying to teach you – about yourself, your life, and His character. Listen to His small voice that knocks your heart today.

The answer to today's Bible question is. "Aramaic." Although Jesus understood all languages.

Prayer: "Dear God, I sometimes forget that I still have a lot to learn. Open my eyes to see and my ears to hear the lessons of Your Truth before me today. Lord, speak to me, and I'll listen. I'm here, Lord; send me to the place and give me the purpose I needed today. Guide me, Lord, daily. Amen."

MORE FROM GOD'S WORD

Psalm 34:11
"Come, ye children, hearken unto me: I will teach you the fear of the LORD."

Psalm 73:24
"Thou shalt guide me with thy counsel, and afterward receive me to glory."

Psalm 143:8
"Cause me to hear thy lovingkindness in the morning; for in thee do I trust: cause me to know the way wherein I should walk; for I lift up my soul unto thee."

The Bible speaks with power and practicality to everything you are facing, thinking, and feeling. The God who seems so distant to you in this moment is actually near and active.
- Paul David Tripp

5 Minute Journaling

ONE THING I WANT TO REMEMBER ABOUT TODAY'S DEVOTION

_____

_____

_____

_____

_____

TODAY I UNDERSTOOD...

_____

_____

_____

_____

_____

TODAY I'M GRATEFUL FOR...

_____

_____

_____

_____

_____

One In Spirit

Fulfil ye my joy, that ye be likeminded, having the same love, being of one accord, of one mind.
Philippians 2:2

FOCUS FOR TODAY

We need to take care of one another to build connections in unity through the Holy Spirit.

Bible question for the day. "Who married Moses"?

One of the joys of team sports is working together to achieve a shared goal. Although some players may play critical roles and serve as leaders, each player becomes significant if the team wins. In the body of Christ, this must be our mindset as well. We have different and unique gifts, skills, and capabilities, but all of us are equally important. When we allow disagreements and differences to define us, we are not pleasing our Father. He wants us to love one another, forgive one another, and work together toward advancing His kingdom. As we collaborate and cooperate, we discover the joy and satisfaction that comes from participating in a cause so much bigger than ourselves.

The gift of having and being in a community is wrapped with our responsibility for handling one another. God encourages us that we need to take care of one another. We must uphold building connection, focusing on building a community in love and deeds. Because of what God has done in our lives, we have more reason to celebrate than a team that just won the Super Bowl or the World Series! We should treat one another accordingly.

The answer to today's Bible question is. "Zipporah."

Prayer: "Dear God, thank you for my brothers and sisters in Christ. I pray that we would reflect on you with our humility, kindness, and love toward one another. Help me forgive the people in my life who hurt me. Grant me peace and allow me, Lord, to experience your love so I can also love others the way you love me. Amen."

MORE FROM GOD'S WORD

1 Corinthians 1:10
"Now I beseech you, brethren, by the name of our Lord Jesus Christ, that ye all speak the same thing, and that there be no divisions among you; but that ye be perfectly joined together in the same mind and in the same judgment."

1 Peter 3:8
"Finally, be ye all of one mind, having compassion one of another, love as brethren, be pitiful, be courteous:"

Acts 2:46-47
"46 And they, continuing daily with one accord in the temple, and breaking bread from house to house, did eat their meat with gladness and singleness of heart, 47 Praising God, and having favour with all the people. And the Lord added to the church daily such as should be saved."

"We are only as strong as we are united, as weak as we are divided."
- J.K. Rowling.

5 Minute Journaling

ONE THING I WANT TO REMEMBER ABOUT TODAY'S DEVOTION

_____

_____

_____

_____

_____

TODAY I UNDERSTOOD...

_____

_____

_____

_____

_____

TODAY I'M GRATEFUL FOR...

_____

_____

_____

_____

_____

Our Firm Foundation

The name of the LORD is a strong tower: the
righteous runneth into it, and is safe.
Proverbs 18:10

FOCUS FOR TODAY

God is our security; we can run to Him anytime.

Bible question for the day. "How many chapters does the book of Judges have?"

More than ever, your world changes not just daily but hourly. Relationships come and go, and new opportunities flash before you while other doors close. Information assaults you from many media sources constantly competing to attract attention. Disaster strikes and tragedies unfold, along with an occasional surprise. With so much change, it's hard to feel as though you're on solid ground. The world can feel like a strange and unfamiliar place from one day to the next.

That is why you can't survive without the firmest foundation for your life. God remains the same regardless of what the stock market does or how many downsize. You can rest in the knowledge that no matter how chaotic and unstable the rest of your life may feel, your relationship with God your Father is rock solid. No matter what happens in the world today, we find peace and comfort that God is our security. We can run to Him anytime as our safe place. People may hurt us; God can cheer us up. Circumstances may disappoint us; God will comfort us. The goodness of the Lord continues to prevail, and we can trust Him in our daily living.

The answer to today's Bible question is. "The book of Judges has 21 chapters."

Prayer: "God, I'm so grateful that You're always the same. The uncertainty of all that can change in life sometimes scares me. But when I remember that You are in control. Thank you, Father, for wrapping me with your righteousness, love & comfort. Amen."

MORE FROM GOD'S WORD

Psalm 18:2
"The LORD is my rock, and my fortress, and my deliverer; my God, my strength, in whom I will trust; my buckler, and the horn of my salvation, and my high tower."

Psalm 61:3
"For thou hast been a shelter for me, and a strong tower from the enemy."

Psalm 144:2
"My goodness, and my fortress; my high tower, and my deliverer; my shield, and he in whom I trust; who subdueth my people under me."

It is not the beauty of a building you should look at; its the construction of the foundation that will stand the test of time.
- Allan Coe

5 Minute Journaling

ONE THING I WANT TO REMEMBER ABOUT TODAY'S DEVOTION

_____

_____

_____

_____

_____

TODAY I UNDERSTOOD…

_____

_____

_____

_____

_____

TODAY I'M GRATEFUL FOR…

_____

_____

_____

_____

_____

Overflowing With Thankfulness

As ye have therefore received Christ Jesus the
Lord, so walk ye in him: Rooted and built up in
him, and stablished in the faith, as ye have been
taught, abounding therein with thanksgiving.
Colossians 2:6-7

FOCUS FOR TODAY

Living with Christ includes overflowing with gratitude.

Bible question for the day. "How did Jesus reveal the one who betrayed Him"?

Sometimes it takes a season of hardship, loss, and suffering to remind us of all we have been given – and to appreciate how God provides. Indeed, the early pilgrims to our country faced struggles far beyond what they imagined in the new, untamed wilderness. Without the help of Native Americans willing to share food and teach them how to farm and hunt, the first colonists would have likely perished in only a few months. But God prepared and brought others into their lives to help them discover survival methods. Their new lifestyle certainly wasn't as easy as they may have hoped, but the Lord strengthened them and provided for them nonetheless. Many early European settlers came to America to have religious freedom and worship God independently.

As a celebration of Thanksgiving begins a season of feasting, celebrating, and partying, let's not lose sight of worshiping together, thanking our Creator for the many ways He has blessed each of us as well as our ancestors.

Many in this world are losing hope as it spins more cruelly out of control. Rarely is truth, justice, and love are found rarely, and they cannot understand it. The Good Shepherd calls to His sheep reaches out His mighty hand. He goes after His strays and rescues His lost. Listen. Jesus is calling you now! Knock on My door and sit by My well lay down your burdens and take My hand to overflow your cup with My piece My angels will protect you My Spirit will guide you I will uplift you on Eagles wings as we walked together each day. God's Spirit is with us. He sets our life before us, so we learn and grow. He reaches out to protect us too often from ourselves. He knows where you are. God has fruitful plans for you! Smiles chastises and suffers with you. He forgives all if you ask and replaces your tears with joy. He loves you. What does Jesus ask? Only two things. To truly love God with all your being and truly love your brothers. Wake up and hear His voice! Be not waylaid by the wolves of this world by diligently and eagerly, with humility. Seek His path and Share His love now before his judgment day must come.

The answer to today's Bible question is. The Lord dipped a piece of bread and passed it to him (Judas)."

Prayer: "Lord, for all the hard times through which You've brought me this year, I thank you. You are always with me and always protect and provide for me. I surrender to you my life, and in the coming days, I'm about to live for you. Help me finish well in this walk, Lord. Amen."

MORE FROM GOD'S WORD

Colossians 4:2
"Continue in prayer, and watch in the same with thanksgiving;"

Psalm 106:1
"Praise ye the LORD. O give thanks unto the LORD; for he is good: for his mercy endureth for ever."

Hebrews 12:28-29
"28 Wherefore we receiving a kingdom which cannot be moved, let us have grace, whereby we may serve God acceptably with reverence and godly fear: 29 For our God is a consuming fire."

"O Lord that lends me life, lend me a heart replete with thankfulness."
- William Shakespeare

5 Minute Journaling

ONE THING I WANT TO REMEMBER ABOUT TODAY'S DEVOTION

_____

_____

_____

_____

_____

TODAY I UNDERSTOOD…

_____

_____

_____

_____

_____

TODAY I'M GRATEFUL FOR…

_____

_____

_____

_____

_____

Pleasing God

But without faith it is impossible to please him: for he that cometh to God must believe that he is, and that he is a rewarder of them that diligently seek him.
Hebrews 11:6

FOCUS FOR TODAY

We only have one audience to please and it's above. It's God.

Bible question for the day. The Bible question for the day. "What chapters in the book of Matthew pertaining to Jesus sermon on the Mount?"

You can never do enough to earn His favor no matter how hard you try to please God. You can give all your money to the church, work on a mission for the homeless, and read your Bible daily. While good if motivated by love and not legalism, these activities are useless when pleasing God unless you have faith.

You naturally rely on them for comfort, connection, and collaboration when you trust someone. Our relationship with God works the same way; it's a relationship, not a business transaction, career opportunity, or magic lamp. No matter what we do, He will be pleased if we do it unto the Lord with sincere faith. But He does want us to grow and mature in our faith. A father cherishes the crayon-drawn picture his daughter draws him, but he expects more when the child grows into an adult. The good news is that we can't force ourselves to grow – it happens naturally as we become more deeply acquainted with the love of our Heavenly Father.

Faith is a gift from God, and we can't earn it. Faith is not just believing but allowing God to reveal to His Spirit and work in us. He will make us grow; we also need to respond to the growth given to us. One way to love God is to obey Him, obeying Him the faith He in birth within us through His word, Spirit, and circumstances.

The answer to today's Bible question is. "The book of Matthew chapter 5 chapter 6 chapter 7".

Prayer: "Thank You for loving me and rewarding me with so many blessings as Your child. Help me live by faith, serving You from my love for You and nothing more. Faith without works is dead. Amen."

FROM GOD'S WORD

Mark 8:34
"And when he had called the people unto him with his disciples also, he said unto them, Whosoever will come after me, let him deny himself, and take up his cross, and follow me."

Matthew 17:20
"And Jesus said unto them, Because of your unbelief: for verily I say unto you, If ye have faith as a grain of mustard seed, ye shall say unto this mountain, Remove hence to yonder place; and it shall remove; and nothing shall be impossible unto you."

1 Peter 5:10
"But the God of all grace, who hath called us unto his eternal glory by Christ Jesus, after that ye have suffered a while, make you perfect, stablish, strengthen, settle you."

"The Lord God called you to Himself as His child. In return, you give God what pleases Him most - YOU PRAISE HIM!"
- Shelena Gr

5 Minute Journaling

ONE THING I WANT TO REMEMBER ABOUT TODAY'S DEVOTION

_____

_____

_____

_____

_____

TODAY I UNDERSTOOD…

_____

_____

_____

_____

_____

TODAY I'M GRATEFUL FOR…

_____

_____

_____

_____

_____

Resurrection Life

**And God hath both raised up the Lord, and
will also raise up us by his own power.
1 Corinthians 6:14**

FOCUS FOR TODAY

Our identity and legacy are in Christ alone.

Bible question for the day. "Who was the mother of King Solomon"?

Occasionally, especially as we get older, we begin to wonder what our legacy will be. What will we have accomplished with our life that we will endure after leaving this earth? Are we truly living out our God-given purpose, or are we settled for less? We tend to let our circumstances dictate how we feel, which influences how we act. When we attach this kind of power to events beyond our control, we set ourselves up for dissatisfaction, disappointment, and discouragement. With this bleak mindset, soon it seems as though nothing matters, that regardless of what we do, it does not change anything. This is not living in the abundant life of the resurrection of Christ. Circumstances remain beyond our control, and our souls will sometimes ache with the painful weight of disappointment. But when our hope is in Christ, we can see beyond our momentary discomfort. We can trust God with our past, present, and future, including our legacy.

The answer to today's Bible question is. "Bathsheba."

One of my favorite stories of interest is the Bible. King David was one of the four authors who wrote Psalms and killed Goliath. Saw Bathsheba one day, and he had to have her; King David had his general Uriah killed in battle at the request of his arms bear that made sure Uriah would go back into the battle where it waxed hot. For the reason when you write, it came back from battle King Solomon tried to get Uriah to sleep with Bathsheba, his wife, to look like Uriah had gotten Bathsheba pregnant. And it was King David who got her pregnant while his top general Uriah was fighting for Israel. There is so much to this story, and you will see God at work. Bathsheba died in childbirth having her son King Solomon. King David was supposed to build the temple of God, but the prophet Nathan came in and shook his bony finger at King David and said that the Lord our God would not let him build his temple; instead, his son, Bathsheba's son, King Solomon will build the temple. And the story goes on and is very interested.

Prayer: "Jesus, thank you for rising from the dead and bringing abundant life. I want to trust You fully, knowing that what I do is meaningful for Your kingdom."

MORE FROM GOD'S WORD

1 Corinthians 15:15-20
"15 Yea, and we are found false witnesses of God; because we have testified of God that he raised up Christ: whom he raised not up, if so be that the dead rise not. 16 For if the dead rise not, then is not Christ raised: 17 And if Christ be not raised, your faith is vain; ye are yet in your sins. 18 Then they also which are fallen asleep in Christ are perished. 19 If in this life only we have hope in Christ, we are of all men most miserable. 20 But now is Christ risen from the dead, and become the firstfruits of them that slept."

Acts 2:24
"Whom God hath raised up, having loosed the pains of death: because it was not possible that he should be holden of it"

John 11:25-26
"25 Jesus said unto her, I am the resurrection, and the life: he that believeth in me, though he were dead, yet shall he live: 26 And whosoever liveth and believeth in me shall never die. Believest thou this?

"For me the most radical demand of Christian faith lies in summoning the courage to say yes to the present risenness of Jesus Christ."
- Brennan Manning

5 Minute Journaling

ONE THING I WANT TO REMEMBER ABOUT TODAY'S DEVOTION

_____

_____

_____

_____

_____

TODAY I UNDERSTOOD…

_____

_____

_____

_____

TODAY I'M GRATEFUL FOR…

_____

_____

_____

_____

Running The Race

**Verily, verily, I say unto you, He that heareth
my word, and believeth on him that sent me,
hath everlasting life, and shall not come into
condemnation; but is passed from death unto life.
John 5: 24**

FOCUS FOR TODAY

Life isn't easy but His grace is enough for us to finish the race.
Don't give up.

Bible question for the day. The Bible question for the day. "What is the sixth commandment?"

Like a runner with sore feet, we often struggle to keep putting one foot in front of others. We are tempted to quit the race of faith during these moments and go our way. We want to pursue selfish pleasures that provide instant gratification instead of resisting temptation by trusting God. Often, the enemy of our souls knows that we are vulnerable and weak, weary and overwhelmed. He may try to lure us away from the path of God's righteousness by throwing simple comforts and addictive idols in front of us.

Running away from the struggles of life never provides relief for long, especially after we have experienced God's goodness. Temptations may appeal to our senses or offer an illusion of rest and comfort. But ultimately, they distract us from what matters most. If we want to run the race of faith, we must be prepared to keep going. And we can't; we must trust God to carry us. We have already crossed the finish line from death to life. It's all done on the cross. God will sustain us as we keep running.

How are you today? Jesus is there for us every step as we run this race. I understand it's tiring. But keep holding. Don't give up. Praying for your healing and holistic wellness. I believe in you. God will make it through.

The answer to today's Bible question is. "Exodus 20; 16. – "Thou shalt not kill."

Prayer: "Lord, I believe that You died for my sins and know that You have secured the prize for me. Please help me keep running the race of faith, one day at a time. Jesus, it's not easy to walk in this life, but please, Lord, sustain and deliver us from any wickedness. Help us finish well. We long to see and be with you in heaven but while we are still on earth, give us comfort, wisdom, and stamina to keep going. Thank you, Lord, for the people you sent us for us to keep going. Lord, we fix our eyes upon you, alone. Please give us the hope that we need, especially when we feel hopeless. Thank you, Lord, for your daily provision. Amen."

MORE FROM GOD'S WORD

Hebrews 12:1
"Wherefore seeing we also are compassed about with so great a cloud of witnesses, let us lay aside every weight, and the sin which doth so easily beset us, and let us run with patience the race that is set before us,"

2 Timothy 4:7
"I have fought a good fight, I have finished my course, I have kept the faith:"

Galatians 5:7
"Ye did run well; who did hinder you that ye should not obey the truth?"

"Remember no matter how fast you run, you can't be the winner if you don't finish. As someone said, to be the first to finish, you must finish first! Go, take the strike!"
- Israelmore Ayivor

5 Minute Journaling

ONE THING I WANT TO REMEMBER ABOUT TODAY'S DEVOTION

_____

_____

_____

_____

_____

TODAY I UNDERSTOOD...

_____

_____

_____

_____

_____

TODAY I'M GRATEFUL FOR...

_____

_____

_____

_____

_____

Seek His Wisdom

Wisdom is good with an inheritance: and by it there is profit to them that see the sun.
Ecclesiastes 7:11

FOCUS FOR TODAY

God's wisdom is always available to us daily.
Pray and seek Him.

Bible question for the day. The Bible question for the day. "Can you name the fifth commandment?"

As children of the King, our inheritance in Christ holds vast riches. Indeed, the priceless gift of our salvation tops the list, but the wisdom that comes from following Jesus is just as precious. When we follow Him, whether the site of many foolish pursuits we once chased after. On a day when fools seem to be celebrated as comical and silly, it's good to remember the value of this invaluable resource.

We benefit like this sapling growing beneath the sunshine as we seek God's wisdom. Wisdom has a larger perspective, and trust God's sovereignty beyond what you can see, hear, and touch. Wisdom provides insight and understanding, compassion and caring. Wisdom emerges from the refining process when you go through the fire. The shallow, superficial things you once worried about are no longer important. You recognize what matters. That's wisdom. Resist the folly of the world and trust in the wisdom of the Lord.

The answer to today's Bible question is. "Exodus 20; 12. - Honor thy father and thy mother; that the days may be long upon the land which the Lord thy God giveth thee."

Prayer: "Father, thank You for the wisdom You gave me when I asked for it and seek Your ways. Guide me, Lord daily. Amen."

MORE FROM GOD'S WORD

Psalm 107:43
"Whoso is wise, and will observe these things, even they shall understand the lovingkindness of the Lord."

Proverbs 1:7
"The fear of the Lord is the beginning of knowledge: but fools despise wisdom and instruction."

Proverbs 3:7
"Be not wise in thine own eyes: fear the Lord, and depart from evil."

As we trust God to give us wisdom for today's decisions, He will lead us a step at a time into what He wants us to be doing in the future.
- Theodore Epp

5 Minute Journaling

ONE THING I WANT TO REMEMBER ABOUT TODAY'S DEVOTION

_____

_____

_____

_____

_____

TODAY I UNDERSTOOD…

_____

_____

_____

_____

TODAY I'M GRATEFUL FOR…

_____

_____

_____

_____

Stand Firm

Therefore, my beloved brethren, be ye stedfast, unmoveable, always abounding in the work of the Lord, forasmuch as ye know that your labour is not in vain in the Lord.
1 Corinthians 15:58

FOCUS FOR TODAY

Though life isn't easy, we are called to be steadfast, and be strong in our Christian faith. Jesus paid it all. None is a waste in Him.

Bible question for the day. "How many blind people did Jesus heal"?

Some days it feels as though nothing goes right. You oversleep, your car breaks down, and you miss the big meeting at work. Even when your day goes smoothly, it can still seem monotonous and tiring. You get catch up and all kinds of busyness, but then at the end of the day, you wonder what you've actually accomplished.

People tend to assess their day based on what they produce, complete, resolve, and check off their lists. However, when we focus on God, we can stand firm when change comes our way and blocks our paths. We can know that everything we do contributes to our Father's master plan, His holy purpose for our lives. Even when we feel as though we didn't accomplish anything on our to-do lists, we are part of something bigger and more meaningful than we can see.

Though life isn't easy, we are called to be steadfast, and be strong in our Christian faith. Jesus paid it all. None is a waste in Him.

The answer to today's Bible question is. "Jesus healed six blind people."

Prayer: Dear God, I get frustrated with how challenging my life seems. Help me to remember that when it's for Your glory, my actions will always have purpose and meaning."

MORE FROM GOD'S WORD

2 Timothy 1; 7
"For God hath not given us the spirit of fear; but of power, and of love, and of a sound mind."

2 Chronicles 15:7
"Be ye strong therefore, and let not your hands be weak: for your work shall be rewarded."

John 14:27
"Peace I leave with you, my peace I give unto you: not as the world giveth, give I unto you. Let not your heart be troubled, neither let it be afraid."

"It is your faith that will make you stand firm."
- Lailah Gifty Akita

5 Minute Journaling

ONE THING I WANT TO REMEMBER ABOUT TODAY'S DEVOTION

_____

_____

_____

_____

_____

TODAY I UNDERSTOOD...

_____

_____

_____

_____

_____

TODAY I'M GRATEFUL FOR...

_____

_____

_____

_____

_____

The Advent

And God is able to make all grace abound toward you; that ye, always having all sufficiency in all things, may abound to every good work:
2 Corinthians 9:8

FOCUS FOR TODAY

The source of our provision will not run out.
It's His grace that abounds daily.

Bible question for the day. "Paul and Silas were imprisoned during the second missionary journey, but in what city did this happen"?

Most home improvement projects take twice as long because the homeowner has to make at least four trips to the hardware store. The first time is to buy the wrong things. The second time is to buy the wrong size. The homeowner buys one of everything and every measure on the third trip. The fourth trip allows them to return all the stuff they did not need.

What would it be like to have exactly what you need for all things at all times to do your work? We cannot even imagine! Yet God promises that when we are doing His excellent work, the work He has given us to do, we will have everything we need. It is called grace. It is not something that we can earn, buy or conjure. It is free from a loving God who wants to give us gifts to do His will. He will surprise this as we do His good works. We might not recognize ourselves, but we will recognize Him. His grace abounds and is sufficient for us daily.

The day before Thanksgiving, most others are busy preparing for family gatherings and purchasing items to have a warm meal and get together. It is the loneliest time for some people because they either have no one to celebrate with, or they have never had a blessed holiday season themselves. Reaching out to the lonely-hearted is a gracious God-given gift to do. Keep in mind 25,000 people every day die of starvation on this planet. Keep them in mind, say prayers, and thank God for the blessings you have been given this holiday season. Because His grace overflows in us, we can also extend this mainly to the needy, hurting, and the lost. When you have God and His grace, you have all you need to give others. We are to be cheerfully given our time, talent, and resources to those in need.

The answer to today's Bible question is. "Philippi"

Prayer: "Father, help me look to You for all I need to do Your will. Thank You for Your gift of grace. Lord, please give me a generous heart that looks out for others' needs. Use me as a consistent conduit, Lord, for your glory. In Jesus name. Amen."

MORE FROM GOD'S WORD

Proverbs 25:11
"A word fitly spoken is like apples of gold in pictures of silver."

James 1:17
"Every good gift and every perfect gift is from above, and cometh down from the Father of lights, with whom is no variableness, neither shadow of turning."

Philippians 4:19
"But my God shall supply all your need according to his riches in glory by Christ Jesus."

It is better to grow in grace than gifts.
- Thomas Watson

5 Minute Journaling

ONE THING I WANT TO REMEMBER ABOUT TODAY'S DEVOTION

_____

_____

_____

_____

_____

TODAY I UNDERSTOOD...

_____

_____

_____

_____

TODAY I'M GRATEFUL FOR...

_____

_____

_____

_____

The Ancient Paths

Thus saith the Lord, Stand ye in the ways, and see,
and ask for the old paths, where is the good way,
and walk therein, and ye shall find rest for your
souls. But they said, We will not walk therein.
Jeremiah 6:16

FOCUS FOR TODAY

God guides and provides.

Bible question for the day. "Why was it important that David killed the giant"?

Since we have GPS applications and map software on phones and tablets – or even installed in our vehicles – few people have to stop while driving and ask others for directions anymore. However, we still benefit from the knowledge and wisdom of other travelers. When we visit a new area of our country or travel overseas, we find consult guidebooks, reviews from other travelers, and recommendations from experts.

Our spiritual journey is the same. We can benefit so much from the hundreds of years of wisdom and experience that other Christians have left us as their legacy. When we read the writings of ancient pilgrims of the faith, we can look into the heart of another brother or sister in Christ. We can understand their struggles, appreciate their insight, and learn from their timeless faith in the Lord. The wisdom of other Christians provided us with a more extensive roadmap on our journey. We can see beyond what we have experienced and realize that we will be stretched and called to venture into unknown territory, places that have already been blazed by other believers who have gone ahead of us. We are never traveling alone.

The answer to today's Bible question is. "If David did not kill the giant, his people would have to serve the giant's people.

Prayer: "Jesus, I'm grateful that Your example provides a North Star by which I can guide my life. Help me to follow You today and all that I do. Guide me, Lord, and pave the road you prepare for me. Amen."

MORE FROM GOD'S WORD

Psalm 37:7
"Rest in the Lord*, and wait patiently for him: fret not thyself because of him who prospereth in his way, because of the man who bringeth wicked devices to pass."*

Psalm 37:5
"Commit thy way unto the Lord*; trust also in him; and he shall bring it to pass."*

Psalm 118:8
"It is better to trust in the Lord *than to put confidence in man."*

"Where God guides, He provides. No matter how things look, God is still in control. Stay in peace and be hopeful. Your blessing is coming soon."
- Germany Kent

5 Minute Journaling

ONE THING I WANT TO REMEMBER ABOUT TODAY'S DEVOTION

_____

_____

_____

_____

_____

TODAY I UNDERSTOOD...

_____

_____

_____

_____

TODAY I'M GRATEFUL FOR...

_____

_____

_____

_____

The Love Of Money

For the love of money is the root of all evil: which while some coveted after, they have erred from the faith, and pierced themselves through with many sorrows.
1 Timothy 6:10

FOCUS FOR TODAY

There's nothing you can save, buy,
or spend that you could take with you for eternity.

Bible question for the day. According to one of the famous Bible quotes, what is the "root of all kinds of evil"?

When the weed takes root in your garden, it drains nutrients in the soil away from other plants, such as flowers or vegetables. Many weeds often bind themselves around the roots of other plants to anchor themselves into the soil deeper. They choke off the different plants and secure themselves into the ground. Eventually, they replace the flower and its natural survival system with its roots, shoots, and tendrils.

The love and pursuit of money can be an enormous weed in our spiritual garden. With thorns that entrapped you and agreed that crows like dandelions, desire for wealth could block your vision, disrupt your path, and kill your heart. The love of money can lead to another person cultivating another sin like greed, discontentment, ungratefulness, and materialism. There's nothing you can save, buy, or spend that you could take with you for eternity. Only the fruit of the Spirit that you cultivate now will last. Spend time today tending your spiritual garden, eliminating the weed of greed.

The answer to today's Bible question is. "The love of money."

Prayer: Dear Father, You provided all my needs and blessed me with everything I have. Protect me from the lure of more money. As I wait and work hard with your blessings, Help me see Lord the beauty of your gifts, provision, and grace in my life. Amen.

MORE FROM GOD'S WORD

Ecclesiastes 5:10
"He that loveth silver shall not be satisfied with silver; nor he that loveth abundance with increase: this is also vanity."

2 Timothy 3:2
"For men shall be lovers of their own selves, covetous, boasters, proud, blasphemers, disobedient to parents, unthankful, unholy,"

Hebrews 13:5
"Let your conversation be without covetousness; and be content with such things as ye have: for he hath said, I will never leave thee, nor forsake thee."

"Don't let affluence make you impoverished of God."
- Jon Bloom

5 Minute Journaling

ONE THING I WANT TO REMEMBER ABOUT TODAY'S DEVOTION

_____

_____

_____

_____

_____

TODAY I UNDERSTOOD...

_____

_____

_____

_____

TODAY I'M GRATEFUL FOR...

_____

_____

_____

_____

The Servant Of All

And he sat down, and called the twelve, and
saith unto them, If any man desire to be first, the
same shall be last of all, and servant of all.
Mark 9:35

FOCUS FOR TODAY

In the eyes of God, the greatest rank is being the
last, which means being in service to others.

Bible question for the day. "Which comes first, Jeremiah or limitations"?

We place a lot of stock in numbers, want to finish first, and know where we rank compared to our peers. Lists are compiled annually of the wealthiest, the most influential, and the most famous. Athletes are used to being tagged, and most businesses rely on numbers to determine their budgets, goals, and margins. Usually, people are only happy when moving up on the list.

However, there is one list that we should hope to be last on; those people who want to be first in the kingdom of God. Jesus tells us that you wish to demonstrate your passion, commitment, and dedication to the Lord. You must be the servant of all – last on the list. In the dog-eat- dog world, where competing means knowing your numerical place, it is not easy to adopt a mindset of servanthood. You are in last means to be a service to others. No one may see how you serve your family, how you do your best to work, how you secretly give to the needy. In the eyes of God, He sees your devotion and good works in the secret place. Pause for a moment and think of the people in the sphere of your influence that needs your grace, kindness, mercy, and service. Today, let Jesus be your role model for being first by being last.

The answer to today's Bible question is. "Jeremiah."

Prayer: "Lord, forgive me for wanting to be first and to compete with those around me. Strengthen my heart to serve You humbly, to be first only by being less. Lord, reveal to me people in my life that I can be a vessel of your love, comfort, and encouragement. Heal and fill me with your Spirit, Lord, so that I can overflow my cup to others. Amen."

MORE FROM GOD'S WORD

Matthew 20:26
"But it shall not be so among you: but whosoever will be great among you, let him be your minister;"

Matthew 23:11
"But he that is greatest among you shall be your servant."

Mark 9:36
"And he took a child, and set him in the midst of them: and when he had taken him in his arms, he said unto them,"

The end of all knowledge should be service to others.
- Cesar Chavez

5 Minute Journaling

ONE THING I WANT TO REMEMBER ABOUT TODAY'S DEVOTION

_____

_____

_____

_____

_____

TODAY I UNDERSTOOD...

_____

_____

_____

_____

_____

TODAY I'M GRATEFUL FOR...

_____

_____

_____

_____

_____

The Trials Into Trophies

For ye are dead, and your life is hid with Christ in God.
Colossians 3:3

FOCUS FOR TODAY

God's grace can turn our wounds into wisdom, trials into trophies, and from being a victim to being a victor.

Bible question for the day. "Judas betrayed Jesus for exactly how many coins of silver?"

When we accept Christ into our lives and follow Him, our sins are forgiven, and our past is buried. However, we often continue living as if our past struggles still have power over us. Like some monster in the story or movie, or mistakes came back to life and seemed to refuse to stay buried. So we keep trying to suppress them and keep them underground - only to find ourselves struggling with them a short time later.

Instead of considering our past mistakes and sinful hideous that we must kill, we would better rethink how we look at things. What if you viewed your past offenses as seeds of redemption, bulbs to be planted in the soil of grace and watered by the love of the Father? You do not have to keep burying seeds and bulbs; you do it once and then wait for them to push through the soil and bring new life. The flowers, buds, and branches that result look nothing like the seeds and bulbs they sprang. God is doing something beautiful from your past. You do not have to run from your old mistakes. You only have to turn them over to the Lord and let the Lord transform them. The deadly sin we have in our lives are all paid through the cross. Let's focus on heavenly and Godly thoughts and the faith God gives us daily.

The answer to today's Bible question is. "30 pieces of silver".

Prayer: "Lord, I'm amazed at how You can redeem my past mistakes and transform my trials into Your trophies. I praise You for Your mercies daily. Help me and give me the heart to fear You and Your righteousness. Lord, I want to seek you above all else. Please give me the wisdom on how I should respond to the trials, temptation, and turbulence in my life. Amen."

MORE FROM GOD'S WORD

Galatians 5:19
"Now the works of the flesh are manifest, which are these; Adultery, fornication, uncleanness, lasciviousness,"

Romans 8:7
"Because the carnal mind is enmity against God: for it is not subject to the law of God, neither indeed can be."

Romans 8:13
"For if ye live after the flesh, ye shall die: but if ye through the Spirit do mortify the deeds of the body, ye shall live."

"Sometimes life takes you into a dark place where you feel it's impossible to breathe. You think you've been buried, but don't give up, because if truth be told, you've actually been planted."
- Karen Gibbs

5 Minute Journaling

ONE THING I WANT TO REMEMBER ABOUT TODAY'S DEVOTION

_____

_____

_____

_____

_____

TODAY I UNDERSTOOD…

_____

_____

_____

_____

_____

TODAY I'M GRATEFUL FOR…

_____

_____

_____

_____

_____

Through His Power

Hatred stirreth up strifes: but love covereth all sins.
Proverbs 10:12

FOCUS FOR TODAY

Forgiving isn't forgetting, but we release the bondage and allow ourselves to grow in suffering.

Bible question for the day. "Who baptizes Jesus?"

When we forgive other people, we display a response that often defies logic. After all, some wrongs seemed too big to be ignored; rape, murder, genocide, etc. However, God forgives all sins – there is not one that's any worse than another, although some sins certainly have more significant, more devastating consequences.

But all have sinned, and we all fall short of the glory of God. When we choose to hate instead of love, we say that only some sins are forgivable. However, that's not what God tells us and shows us through His grace. He sent Christ to live among us and die on the cross for our sins. Our Father wanted us to see His love in action irrefutable, revocable way. Christ's death and resurrection changed everything. We aren't limited by our hatred or inability to love. We can love even those who hurt us with unimaginable betrayals and injuries through God's power.

Do not be a prisoner in your mind of people, places, or things renting space. Releasing and forgiving people aren't easy, but this is what God commanded us. It doesn't mean we tolerate the behavior and injustice but release and allow God's justice to vindicate us. God sees your heart, struggle, pain, and rejection, and He will absolve you. You may be tempted to rebel and fight others. Be still; God will do on your behalf. We need to give Him our hearts and hurt so He can pour out His love and comfort to us. Forgiving isn't forgetting, but we release the bondage and allow ourselves to grow in suffering.

The answer to today's Bible question is. "John the Baptist."

Prayer: Heavenly Father, Your love and grace cover all sins, not just a few. Help me show the same passion and acceptance to everyone, no matter their sins." Father God, we humbly ask for the healing power of Your Spirit. Lord, search my heart who are the people in my life I need to forgive and give me strength to love and forgive them through Jesus Christ our Lord. Amen."

MORE FROM GOD'S WORD

Matthew 6:14
"For if ye forgive men their trespasses, your heavenly Father will also forgive you:"

Colossians 3:13
"Forbearing one another, and forgiving one another, if any man have a quarrel against any: even as Christ forgave you, so also do ye."

Matthew 18:21-22
"21 Then came Peter to him, and said, Lord, how oft shall my brother sin against me, and I forgive him? till seven times? 22 Jesus saith unto him, I say not unto thee, Until seven times: but, Until seventy times seven."

In the shadow of my hurt, forgiveness feel like a decision to reward my enemy. But in the shadow of the cross, forgiveness is merely a gift from one undeserving soul to another.
- Andy Stanley,

Forgiveness will help you more than the person you forgive.
- Catherine Pulsiferbbs

5 Minute Journaling

ONE THING I WANT TO REMEMBER ABOUT TODAY'S DEVOTION

_____

_____

_____

_____

_____

TODAY I UNDERSTOOD…

_____

_____

_____

_____

TODAY I'M GRATEFUL FOR…

_____

_____

_____

_____

True Abundance

**Grace and peace be multiplied unto you through
the knowledge of God, and of Jesus our Lord,
2 Peter 1:2**

FOCUS FOR TODAY

Jesus fills our cup with an abundance of grace and peace.

Bible question for the day. "Who went with Paul on his first missionary journey?"

In our consumer culture, we are often encouraged to buy in bulk. Big-box stores offer low prices on products that can be sold in multiple units. As a result, many people stock up on staples and end up with a year's worth of paper towels, canned tomatoes, or apple juice. We even have TV shows about people who excel at using coupons to save money and acquire more products. And taken to an extreme (as if it's not already), we see cases with people who horrid things they will never use, acquiring more and more out of compulsion.

True abundance, of course, is not about having more stuff. It doesn't rely on stockpiling canned goods, paper products, or emergency candles to light up a stadium. True abundance is not about the number of material possessions you have but the quality of your heart and soul. When we dwell on our knowledge of God and His Son, we experience an abundance of peace and grace. We don't have to have more to experience the satisfaction and joy that only our Lord can provide.

It's not what you can accumulate along this journey that matters; it is who you are in your heart and your soul. We came into this world with absolutely nothing, and the short time we are here as compared to eternity, we are leaving the same way. Please read the Bible; it is the word of God, inspired by the Holy Spirit that Jesus Christ our Lord left us with, Before ascending into heaven. God through the Holy Spirit inspired the writers of God's word. Approximately 40 authors. God does not make mistakes. And God does not make junk.

Recommendation: with the Bible, for this reason, it may seem overwhelming. Psalms 23. 1 Corinthians 13, The book of "James." Jesus Christ our Lord's sermon on the Mount. "Matthew chapter 5, 6, and 7". Psalms 91. "John 3; 16. – For God so loved the world, He gave His only begotten Son, that whosoever shall believe in Him should not perish, but have everlasting life. These are real short reads and possibly give a simplified version and spark interest. "Psalms 22". It was written approximately 1000 years before the birth of Christ. Isaiah 53". It was written approximately 400 years before the birth of Christ. There is boundless wisdom and knowledge through the word of God, like music to the soul and soothing to the heart. Not to mention theword. "Truth." is Indisputable for those with faith and their spiritual eyes wide open. Faith without works is dead. Prayer is powerful medicine and fasting. It shows God that you love him, and The Lord will answer prayers.

The brevity of life is like spokes through a keyhole. This is a one-on-one deal is no getting out of this life except through death and dying, and standing in front of Jesus Christ our Lord who is seated at the right hand of God the Father Almighty awaiting to judge the living and the dead. We will be judged on our thoughts on our words, what we do and what we fail to do.

The answer to today's Bible question is. "Barnabas

Prayer: "Lord, I have all that I need for today. Thank You for meeting all my needs and providing me with many blessings. Amen."

MORE FROM GOD'S WORD

John 10:10
"The thief cometh not, but for to steal, and to kill, and to destroy: I am come that they might have life, and that they might have it more abundantly."

Matthew 6:33
"But seek ye first the kingdom of God, and his righteousness; and all these things shall be added unto you."

Psalm 16:11
"Thou wilt shew me the path of life: in thy presence is fulness of joy; at thy right hand there are pleasures for evermore."

"God will overflow your cup, so grab the biggest one you can find."
- Rob Liano

5 Minute Journaling

ONE THING I WANT TO REMEMBER ABOUT TODAY'S DEVOTION

_____

_____

_____

_____

_____

TODAY I UNDERSTOOD...

_____

_____

_____

_____

_____

TODAY I'M GRATEFUL FOR...

_____

_____

_____

_____

_____

Ultimate Authority

According as his divine power hath given unto us all
things that pertain unto life and godliness, through the
knowledge of him that hath called us to glory and virtue:
2 Peter 1:3

FOCUS FOR TODAY

We are fully equipped to live a Godly life what He calls us for
His glory.

Bible question for the day. "From what tribe of Israel did the apostle Paul come from"?

A person with absolute power and authority never needs to bully anyone. They rest in confidence, knowing what they can do if necessary to accomplish the responsibilities. These people are often natural leaders who inspire confidence in the people around them. They respect others and earn their followers respect, rather than demanding it because of title, rank, or position.

God holds ultimate authority and will always be more powerful than anyone or anything we can imagine. Yet He yields His power and holiness with compassion and mercy, patiently pursuing us when we stray and guiding us in His ways. God is not a bully or dictator. He's a loving Father. Welcome the opportunities to obey God today as ways to recognize and honor His glorious authority and grace-filled power.

Today, ask others around you if there's anything you can do for them or anything they may need. And let others know that you care about them, that you're proud of them. God's gift to us is life; what we do with this life is our gift to God. God bless with love and prayers. With Christ, we are not missing anything. We are fully equipped, but we also need to do our part to partner with God with His Spirit and our effort to obey.

The answer to today's Bible question is. "The tribe of Benjamin."

Prayer: "Oh, Lord, I'm humbled and amazed when I consider Your vast power and infinite mercy. Thank you for how You wheeled them together as my loving Father."

MORE FROM GOD'S WORD

Romans 15:13
"Now the God of hope fill you with all joy and peace in believing, that ye may abound in hope, through the power of the Holy Ghost."

John 17:3
"And this is life eternal, that they might know thee the only true God, and Jesus Christ, whom thou hast sent."

Philippians 3:8
"Yea doubtless, and I count all things but loss for the excellency of the knowledge of Christ Jesus my Lord: for whom I have suffered the loss of all things, and do count them but dung, that I may win Christ,"

"There is no army, no fortress, no giant that can stand against our God. No one. I have seen his might with my own eyes."
- Connilyn Cossette

5 Minute Journaling

ONE THING I WANT TO REMEMBER ABOUT TODAY'S DEVOTION

_____

_____

_____

_____

_____

TODAY I UNDERSTOOD…

_____

_____

_____

_____

_____

TODAY I'M GRATEFUL FOR…

_____

_____

_____

_____

_____

Walk In The Light

Blessed is the people that know the joyful sound: they shall walk, O Lord, in the light of thy countenance.
Psalm 89: 15

FOCUS FOR TODAY

Jesus is our living hope and the light of our weary soul.
Walk-in Him.

Bible question for the day. The Bible question for the day. "Which of the following are not one of the first four books of the New Testament"? Mark Matthew Luke James John?"

When the electricity goes out, when the flashlight doesn't work, when night falls faster than we thought on our hike, we experience darkness in an entirely new way. We may be tempted to panic and wonder how we will see and be able to keep going. We may trip or stumble, groping around in the dark to find candles or fresh batteries. Even after our eyes adjust to the darkness, we may still struggle to see.

Sometimes we become so burdened with the cares of life that it feels as though the lights have dimmed around us. Circumstances seem bleak, and we can't see clearly as darkness seems to close in around us. We struggle for more light, for a clearer sense of what's going on. During these periods of darkness, we must rely on God's light, trusting that it's there even if we can't see it the way we want. Like the sun or stars absurd by cloud cover, the light remains even though it's not visible. We simply have to wait for the clouds to pass in order for the light to shine brighter again.

Whatever you are feeling today, wake up and smell the roses, far better than wearing the thorns. When darkness comes, remember it's not yet the end of the tunnel. Jesus is our living hope and the light of our weary soul. Walk-in Him.

The answer to today's Bible question is. "James".

Prayer: "Dear Lord, thank You that You are the light of the world. Even when my life seems to grow dark, I know that You are with me. Thank you, Lord, for teaching me to be courageous. I pray for you to remove any anxieties in my life. Restore me, Lord, and guide me daily. Amen."

MORE FROM GOD'S WORD

1 John 1:5
"This then is the message which we have heard of him, and declare unto you, that God is light, and in him is no darkness at all."

Revelation 18:1
"And after these things I saw another angel come down from heaven, having great power; and the earth was lightened with his glory."

Ezekiel 43:2
"And, behold, the glory of the God of Israel came from the way of the east: and his voice was like a noise of many waters: and the earth shined with his glory."

The nearer you take anything to the light, the darker its spots will appear; and the nearer you live to God, the more you will see your own utter vileness.
- Robert Murray McCheyne

5 Minute Journaling

ONE THING I WANT TO REMEMBER ABOUT TODAY'S DEVOTION

_____

_____

_____

_____

_____

TODAY I UNDERSTOOD…

_____

_____

_____

_____

_____

TODAY I'M GRATEFUL FOR…

_____

_____

_____

_____

_____

We Can Handle It

The Lord **is good, a strong hold in the day of trouble;
and he knoweth them that trust in him.**
Nahum 1:7

FOCUS FOR TODAY

God is our most excellent helper in times of
trouble. We can trust Him daily.

Bible question for the day. "For how many days and nights was Jonah in the belly of the great fish"?

It can be hard to sort out all you feel when your heart is troubled. And it can be harder still to know what to do with those emotions. You do not want to unleash them on those around you, who you care about. But you know you cannot keep them bottled up inside. And God does not want you to bury them – that is how bitterness, jealousy, and envy sprout into your life.

Whatever it is, God wants you to share it with Him. Lay down your burden before Him, knowing that He can always handle what you cannot. If you're willing to face your feelings and examine the people and events to which they are connected, it's easier, to be honest before God. On the other hand, when you stuff them, ignore them, or deny them, you set yourself up for much more significant problems. So turn your cares over to God today. Feel today's weight lifted from your shoulders.

Nahum was a Jewish prophet whose name meant comforter or consolation. God is just, jealous and holy. He is also protective and redemptive. While we fear God for He is, we must remember that He is good and our stronghold in the moments of our distress. He is our fortress in this broken world.

The answer to today's Bible question is. "Jonah was in the great fish belly for three days."

The Bible does not say a whale or a shark. God specifically designed a great fish to take Jonah back to Nineveh. Where God had instructed Jonah to go in the first place to minister the word to that wonderful wicked city, Jonah thought he would take a cruise on a luxury liner in the opposite direction. Running from Yahweh was not a good choice. Jonah walked to Jaffa and got a ticket on a luxury liner to Tarshish. A massive storm arises, and the sailors, realizing that it is no ordinary storm, cast lots and discover that Jonah is to blame. Jonah admits this and states that the storm will cease if he is thrown overboard. At first, the sailors ignore Jonah's request and are finally forced to throw Jonah overboard. As a result, the storm calms down, and Jonah is miraculously saved by being swallowed by a giant fish whose belly he spends three days and three nights. Jonah prays to God in his affliction, and in doing so, God commands the great fish to vomit Jonah out. Then God again commands Jonah to travel to Nineveh and prophecy to its inhabitants. This time Jonah reluctantly goes into the city, crying, "in 40 days, Nineveh shall be overthrown." What is Jonas's message to the Ninevites? Even the king of Nineveh puts on sackcloth and sits in ashes, making a proclamation and degrees fasting for the entire large city of Nineveh. The Ninevites were the most wicked people recorded throughout history; they would do things like throw babies into the air catching them with their swords. And other things so atrocious it's not even worth mentioning. Jonah makes the trip from the shore where the great fish vomits them up to Nineveh and one day and usually takes three days with the rapid pace of walking. The entire city, including the king listens to Jonah and turns from their wicked ways.

Prayer: "Lord, I don't want to act on my feelings or let them control my decisions, but I can't ignore them either. Help me express them constructively. Thank you, Lord, that you are just and righteous God Who sees my struggle and suffering. I don't want to take revenge, Lord, but I surrender everything into your hands through your power. Thank you, Lord, for being my stronghold when I feel afraid, troubled with my enemies. Thank you for the healing that you are about to do in my life and the redemptive work you are about to do. It's not easy, but I trust you, Lord. Amen."

MORE FROM GOD'S WORD

2 Corinthians 10:3-4
"3 For though we walk in the flesh, we do not war after the flesh: 4 (For the weapons of our warfare are not carnal, but mighty through God to the pulling down of strong holds;)"

2 Samuel 22:3
"The God of my rock; in him will I trust: he is my shield, and the horn of my salvation, my high tower, and my refuge, my saviour; thou savest me from violence."

Psalm 43:2
"For thou art the God of my strength: why dost thou cast me off? why go I mourning because of the oppression of the enemy?"

"It's a reminder that God is always, always there. He's our rock, our strength, our refuge. And when we can't find even a minuscule trace of His handprint in what we're going through, He's reminding us that He's still there. And He always will be. No matter what."
- Diane Moody

5 Minute Journaling

ONE THING I WANT TO REMEMBER ABOUT TODAY'S DEVOTION

_____

_____

_____

_____

_____

TODAY I UNDERSTOOD…

_____

_____

_____

_____

_____

TODAY I'M GRATEFUL FOR…

_____

_____

_____

_____

_____

Who We Know

**O Lord, be gracious unto us; we have waited
for thee: be thou their arm every morning, our
salvation also in the time of trouble.**
Isaiah 33:2

FOCUS FOR TODAY

God is our strength in this stressful world.

Bible question for the day. "How many times did Jesus miraculously help the apostles catch fish"?

Strength remains a commodity we desire, whether physical, emotional, or spiritual. And in most cases, we know that the kind of strength we desire won't happen overnight. We lift weights and exercise, knowing that we won't be looking like a superhero for some time. We pushed for painful disappointments and agreed on private losses, feeling our emotions but not allowing them to overpower us. And spiritually strengthen our faith by praying, spending time in God's Word, and serving others. However, our spiritual strength isn't built on what we do but on, Who we know. God is the source of our power, and it's our relationship with Him increases our strength, not any spiritual disciplines by themselves. If we are committed to loving God, they are natural ways to flex the muscles of our hearts.

If we are prideful and think it's about us, we are in trouble. Pride was Satan's downfall from heaven, thinking he was better than God. Forgive yourself because you're worth it, and God is proud of you. God does not make junk, and God does not make mistakes. Society is taking a moral downfall by eliminating the laws of God and changing the rules more for man's desires. Jeremiah 13; 10. – "These evil people, who refuse to hear my words, which talk in the imagination of their heart, and walk after other gods, to serve them, and to worship them, shall even be as this girdle, which is good for nothing." Signs of the times of the end are before us. The spiritually blind without faith, has an eternal destination. "hell." The road to hell is wide and paved with bad intentions, and many therefore go burrowing their way in blindly. Yet accepting Jesus is the answer to this. He is our savior. Heaven awaits us. Thus, we need to build and receive Him today as our savior.

God is never changing, and the world is moving forward rapidly at a very narcissistic lustful path, leading to the antichrist. Right now, everything is okay if you have your spiritual eyes wide open, walking that narrow path. Having sex nowadays is like buying a hamburger at

McDonald's, and there are consequences. Fornication sex outside of marriage is a sin and an abomination against God.

2 Corinthians 5; 7. – For we walk by faith, not sight. It's not how much we can collect along this journey; it's who we become and finding our calling through the Holy Spirit from God. Confessing and forsaking your sins, never to do them again, is walking with Jesus Christ, our Lord who went to the cross and shed his precious blood for our wretched sins. Everyone will die, and everyone will stand before the Lord for judgment, on our thoughts, on our words, what we do, and what we fail to do. Making New Year's resolutions and turning your life around walking that narrow path, miracles will happen, and you will know the joy, peace, and happiness that you have never known before and become more Christlike. You may feel hopeless, defeated in this world. God is your oasis and strength in this world.

The answer to today's Bible question is. "Two times."

Prayer: "Lord, I know that my strength relies on You as its source. I pray that I will continue to exercise the strength I find in You and not become prideful of my efforts. Forgive me, Lord, for I often use my effort to fulfill the desire of my flesh. I accept and repent today, asking for your grace, mercy, and strength to renew. Help me have a heart that reveres, delights, and seeks you first and foremost. Amen".

MORE FROM GOD'S WORD

1 Peter 5:6-7
"6 Humble yourselves therefore under the mighty hand of God, that he may exalt you in due time: 7 Casting all your care upon him; for he careth for you."

Psalm 86:17
"Shew me a token for good; that they which hate me may see it, and be ashamed: because thou, LORD, hast holpen me, and comforted me."

Matthew 5:4
"Blessed are they that mourn: for they shall be comforted."

"With God, you are stronger than your struggles and more fierce than your fears. God provides comfort and strength to those who trust in Him. Be encouraged, keep standing, and know that everything's going to be alright."
- Germany Kent

5 Minute Journaling

ONE THING I WANT TO REMEMBER ABOUT TODAY'S DEVOTION

_____

_____

_____

_____

_____

TODAY I UNDERSTOOD…

_____

_____

_____

_____

_____

TODAY I'M GRATEFUL FOR…

_____

_____

_____

_____

_____

Printed in the United States
by Baker & Taylor Publisher Services